Power, Sexuality & Gender Dynamics At Work

Roop Sen | Uma Chatterjee

ATLANTIC
PUBLISHERS & DISTRIBUTORS (P) LTD

ATLANTIC
PUBLISHERS & DISTRIBUTORS (P) LTD

7/22, Ansari Road, Darya Ganj, New Delhi
Tel.: +91-11-4077 5252, 2327 3880
E-mail: orders@atlanticbooks.com
Web: www.atlanticbooks.com

Published by Atlantic Publishers & Distributors (P) Ltd 2024

Previously Published by SAGE Publications in 2021

Printed & bound in India by Atlantic Print Services

Advance Praise

This book is a 'must-read' for every HR professional before they enter the industry. It is filled with thoughtful case studies and the nuances of the matters of the parties involved—the policy makers, the organizations with its POSH and ICC, and the employees. The issue is that while we are all aware, gap between awareness and action is a big one. Communication and awareness at the employee level will build the right culture in an organization. A fascinating read. Just outstanding!

S. V. Nathan, *Partner and Chief Talent Officer, Deloitte India*

A book that provokes, invites, challenges, questions and cleverly takes us to engage with the many shades of grey....

At a time when the world seems polarized into right and wrong, good and bad and when setting up of boundaries has resulted in 'othering', this book is an invitation to have a dialogue and to create spaces of exploration, self-reflection and discovery. The book pushes us into examining the frames we use to view sexual harassment, diversity, gender and sexuality. The stories sound familiar and every day and describe a phenomenon prevalent in our context and raise questions around ethical dilemmas. While the book focuses on corporates, the questions that the authors raise are more universal—the role of structure, laws, friends, bystanders, leadership in understanding the dynamics of power, the dichotomy of espoused values and values in action, understanding boundaries, enabling safe spaces and understanding consent.

Vandana Menon, *Director and Principal Consultant, FLAME TAO Knoware Pvt. Ltd*

A book that provides a refreshing look into and then *much beyond* the question of how to make workplaces safe from sexual harassment. The authors take us, with engaging and complex narratives, into a different scenario—the corporate sector in the urban Indian economy. The book could be a valuable resource for organizations wanting to reflect on how to go above and beyond the mandated framework of internal complaints committees and of signed policies that guide professional behaviour. It asks important questions about how we can build resilient and fulfilling work relationships within highly diverse organizations, where shifts in the normal expectations of gender are happening fast. It highlights the value of open conversations rather than only a rule-based culture around these issues. It looks at the roles and decisions of those affected by a difficult, 'inappropriate' or predatory relationship. It also looks at the impact of the 'bystanders' whose reactions, often gossip, have an important role in setting organizational culture. Although the case studies are more relevant to cultures in India, the questions raised by the case studies and by your analysis in the book would be of interest here, in Europe and the USA too. The questions have implications for people from different nationalities working together and trying to develop working relationships across very different cultures. I would highly recommend reading and using the book to those in HR and leadership roles, as well as others who are simply interested in the future of inclusive, fair and fulfilling workplaces.

Ginny Baumann, *Senior Program Manager, International Development and Human Rights, UK*

This book will count as a significant addition to a collection on understanding sexual harassment at the workplace. It is premised on viewing organizations as human collectives that engender relationships rather than as mere vehicles of performance translating vision and goals into reality. It brings alive the dynamics and fluidity of relationships, the inherent power inequities that operate beneath and set the stage for many a case of sexual harassment at the workplace. Internal mechanisms including legally mandated committees have limitations and often are manned by people ill-trained for this purpose. The authors lay emphasis on regular intra-organization dialogue and openness to bring up issues and deal with infringements as means to foster a shared understanding and acceptance of workplace behaviours, besides becoming a key element of culture shaping. It is an eminently readable book and will serve as reference material for workshops on gender relations and the role of power, hierarchy, consent and culture in shaping notions of what conduct is appropriate, what is violation or harassment and how to engage with issues that arise from the relationships amongst sexes.

K. S. Narendran, *Co-Founder and Director,*
Reflexive Lenses Consulting Pvt. Ltd

Power, Sexuality and Gender Dynamics at Work describes how power dynamics weave its way into our professional lives. It is equally fearsome and fascinating to explore the multiple ways in which internal corporate systems allow and therefore encourage some individuals to insidiously exercise their power using and abusing the values inherent to the companies they work for. Beyond the thoroughness in the description of scenes and the gallery of portraits, Uma Chatterjee and Roop Sen allow us to see the meandering of workplaces when the collective unconscious becomes permeable and shows the individual's experiences with cultural and family dysfunctions in relation to gender dynamics. Mindful of keeping the balance between power and assertiveness, the authors encourage us to think through the characters' own questioning and from the perspectives of both, the one who has the power and the one who perceives the shadows of the abuse. This insightful book is largely evocative of stakes too often present in working environment beyond cultural identities, in Europe as much as in India.

Karine Le Roch, *PhD in Clinical Psychology*

The book touches upon many intersections of polarization in society today, between man and woman, masculinity and femininity, work and life, body and mind, local and global, victim and perpetrator, power and love, reality and ideology, and many more.

It unfolds our personal and collective dilemma, and makes it possible to deconstruct complex issues and therefore work them through. It encourages readers to look at the issues, discuss them and makes it a door that leads to deepen understanding.

It peels off masks of 'professionalism', 'appropriateness', 'political correctness', 'gender neutrality' and 'activism', and guides the readers to listen to true, real, authentic voices beneath the carpet, which will be the path to hope of inclusivity.

This book treats case studies systemically and not individually, which guides the reader to learn that the issue is influenced by the complexity of generations, cultures, social psyche and the history of the organization.

Throughout the book, there are spaces for all, including inconvenient truths. The authors have walked the talk with what they have written.

Yuri Morikawa, *Executive Coach; Organization Development Professional; and Founder, Global Sensation*

Both Chatterjee and Sen have been very keen observers of culture, gender and power relations that are shaping women's experience of their workplaces. They have a natural ability to think critically and unstitch the existing concepts around issues of discrimination and exclusion based on unreasonable biases at workplaces. Having listened closely to women's vulnerabilities as part of their active careers in the development sector, they have experience in helping women navigate out of fear of power through negotiation and leadership. I would have also thought that having been closely associated with injustices towards vulnerable women for most of their lives, their natural sympathies will show bias towards women but I was wrong.

Naghma Mulla, *Chief Operating Officer, EdelGive Foundation*

A book that makes you sit up, look around you (yes, getting taken aback is to be expected, thank Roop!) and understand the enormity of the dynamics of sex, gender, sexuality and power in the workplace. Undergirding these are the menacing tones of violence and violation. Roop is simultaneously forthright and provocative, yet beautifully holds out hope that firmly eschews tokenistic lure but is authentic and substantive. To touch this treasure of hope, this beckoning is to go farther and deeper than 'check-the-box' versions of diversity and inclusion practices and to look the societal and institutional codings and structures right in the eye. The book does something unusual for readers, it offers us a dare! Read it, and I beseech you, take up the dare and help shape the context as it emerges.

Kartikeyan V., *Founder Trustee, Institution for Wholeness & Integration (IWI); Author of* Discover the Alchemist Within—Taking the First Step Towards Personal Growth; *and Co-Architect of the Transformative Alignment Map (TAM©)*

“

To

All those who dare to speak

for themselves and for others

”

Contents

Foreword

In the world of cricket, it is often said that wicketkeepers are noticed only when they drop a catch or miss a stumping opportunity. The same can be said about sexuality in workspaces—it is noticed only when there is a mishap. This insightful book is a great reminder of the all too pervasive presence of sexuality in workspaces. It also goes beyond the obvious factors such as gender discrimination, unconscious bias and LGBT rights and takes the discourse to areas which get lost in the preoccupation with blatant transgression. The real-life case histories chosen by the authors are so 'normal' that one scarcely pays much attention to them, except of course when the people involved decide to 'make an issue'; and when they do, as in these cases, they encounter surprise and hostility, with very little empathy.

Even more remarkably, in most of these cases, sexuality is latent and not explicit. Thus, the protagonists themselves find it difficult to make sense of their unease— 'am I making too much out of it? Perhaps it was just a harmless gesture, or have I invited this onto myself, etc.' These are the host of questions which they struggle with. The ambiguous nature of the encounter makes it very difficult to have a clear opinion and judgement. If an older male boss keeps creating opportunities to spend time with his younger female subordinate, nothing 'inappropriate' has happened. Yet, deep down, the woman 'knows' that she is being used as an object of sexual gratification. How does one decide as to what is appropriate and what is not? How does one decide about what constitutes consent? What should be the response of the system in dealing with these ambiguous situations? What is personal and what is not? These are questions to which there can be no clear answers, and yet they cannot be ignored either. The authors do not try to provide answers but merely provide a perspective and nudge us to think about them.

Whenever people of different genders (and sexual orientations) come together, some sexual energy is triggered. It is not always overt and may not even be experienced by the people as having anything to do with sexuality. Often, it manifests itself in a subtle manner such as heightened self-consciousness, preoccupation with how one is being received, subtle competitiveness with people of one's own gender and shifts in language/body postures. Even without realizing, we also convey messages about our gender ideology. For example, when a woman speaks in soft tones and keeps her gaze down, she conveys a strong adherence to prescribed gender roles. On the other hand, when a woman talks in a loud voice, uses rough language and looks other people in the eye, she communicates her indifference/defiance of prevalent gender roles. These 'unstated statements' generate feeling responses in others, including attraction, repulsion, anger/hostility or tenderness/protective instinct.

Given these complexities, it becomes extremely difficult to differentiate between sexual misconduct (inappropriate action) and sexual exploitation (use of positional power to gain sexual advantage) as evidenced in several case histories cited in this book. Since a large part of the game called sexuality is covert in nature, it is highly 'accident prone'. Very few women would blatantly seduce, and very few men would directly woo or coerce. While in some cases the transactions are direct and explicit, in most others, they are implied and hence subject to the ability of the parties to read each other's message accurately. Just as there are women who complain that their acts of friendship were wrongly interpreted as 'come on' signals, there are many men who feel surprised that what they considered 'consensual arrangement' had many other strings attached to it.

Inaccurate understanding of the other and also confusion in one's own needs and desires, often makes both men and women act in inappropriate ways. While many of these misconducts have elements of sexual exploitation, not all of them do. Admittedly, there is a very thin dividing line between sexual misconduct and sexual exploitation, but it is important to differentiate between the two. A lewd comment and a rape may stem from the same seed of 'male entitlement', but putting the two together in the same basket desensitizes us about the severity of rape.

The main difficulty which arises in differentiating between sexual misconduct and exploitation is in the way sexuality is configured in our minds. There is a strong association of dominance and submission with sexuality. This is equally applicable to 'same-sex relationships'. For example, in the popular film *Three Idiots*, the friends of the protagonist acknowledge his superiority by 'offering' their backside to him. Thus, powerful men tend to assume a certain 'sexual entitlement', and many women in a less powerful position often assume 'sexual obligation'. A certain amount of resistance by the woman is not just treated as 'par for the course' but is also held as desirable. It is also believed that it is the job of the male to overcome this resistance either through wooing or through force. Since men are assumed to be more promiscuous than women, unwarranted sexual initiatives by men are likely to make a woman feel violated (e.g., expressions such as outraging the modesty of the woman). Also, unwarranted sexual initiatives by a woman may be seen as offensive and disgusting but not as outraging the modesty of a man. The sexual act is often seen as a 'means to an end' for a woman and an 'end in itself' for a man.

Also, gender is mostly seen through the binary of man/woman or masculine/feminine. A man with feminine leanings invites disdain, and a woman with greater masculine orientation invites aggression and hostility. This, in turn, creates difficulty in understanding and gracing diverse sexual orientations.

Many of these associations are a product of long human history, particularly of an era when gender roles were clearly segregated, and there was very little need for men and women to share their spaces of work. Today's reality is different, but these associations cannot be simply wished away. They continue to influence our feelings and action, leading to a gap between our rational understanding of ourselves and our deeper feelings and actual behaviour. This gap is often labelled as 'unconscious bias' and becomes a source of guilt and shame for the person. The consequence of this process is that the individual becomes even more defensive. Hence, rather than acknowledging, accepting and working with these associations, the individual denies them even more, making it very difficult to transcend them.

Organizations also contribute to this process by advocating a gender agnostic ideology, i.e., everyone should be treated as a person, not as a man or a woman or that gender does not matter, only skills and competencies are important, etc. In this scenario, people begin to believe that they do not carry any associations with respect to gender differences and that their behaviour is not impacted by gender. The worst part of this approach is that equality is confused with sameness, which in turn leads to insensitivity towards gender differences.

Workspaces are formed, nourished and fostered by communities of gendered beings and not by de-sexualized robots of skills and competencies. They bring their needs, emotions and beliefs including associations around sexuality and gender roles into workspaces. It is neither feasible nor, perhaps, desirable to make workspaces sexually sterile. Whether we acknowledge it or not, sexuality plays (and will continue to do so) an important part in the human dynamics of workspaces. The only meaningful choice that we have is to recognize that today we are required to learn something which our ancestors did not need to, namely, how to share our workspaces with members of other gender(s). This will entail recognizing and celebrating gender differences rather than hiding behind the convenient cloak of 'personhood'. It will also require us to learn to deal with the sexual energy, which will necessarily be triggered by this togetherness, in a mature and dignified manner.

I hope this book will make a significant contribution in this endeavour.

Ashok Malhotra
Managing Director, Reflexive Lenses Consulting;
Co-Founder, Sumedhas,
Academy for Human Context

Preface

The way India and Indian society have dealt with sexual violence, harassment and discrimination can be traced back over the past 50-odd years where women have formed an increasingly large part of the workforce. Corporate environments that were earlier almost completely populated by males have undergone waves of change in their prevailing demographics as well as in their interpretation of 'organizational culture' and value systems. The changing gender ratio in corporate workplaces has resulted in 'corporatization' of these spaces, as increasing diversity in workplaces has increased the demand on organizations to have standard processes and practices that cater to all.

When corporatizing workspaces, organizations create policies and common code of conduct in keeping with the social and organizational culture and laws on the land that employees are expected to follow. However, employees, when they come from diverse cultures and communities, carry personal values and beliefs that they have internalized from their families and societies that they have grown up in, which may or may not always be aligned to the espoused values of the organization. This leads to situations where people are either forced to conform to organizational values that they do not necessarily own, generating conflict and stress, or the organization coping with it by creating a split between espoused values and values in action. Espoused values are those that the organization adopts because they are politically correct, or it believes that those values are good and should be followed. Values in action are those values which are in reality practised by the people and the organization. In environments where conflicting values exist, organizations often avoid dealing with the root of the split, and the leaks are dealt with through band-aids.

The discourse surrounding corporatization brings us to the concept of 'diversity' and 'safety', whose definitions are still elusive in ever-evolving corporate workplaces. How can organizations define these terms to put in place the norms, practices and hierarchies that are acceptable to all? Further, how do organizations define their own 'cultures' and 'values'? We see that increasingly, organizations laud themselves for being 'inclusive' and 'meritocratic', amongst other self-descriptors, but rarely go into what these terms actually mean. What do we mean when we talk about 'inclusion'? How do we deal with boundaries between 'inclusion' and its implied 'exclusion'? Nowadays, when we talk about gender with the background of sexual orientation visibilization, decriminalization and legalization movements, it comes down to managing the same in the workplace. HR departments play a prominent role, and the reality that we are grappling within workplaces is how to actually be diverse and inclusive. Does diversity mean affirmative action and representation in recruitment? Does it mean encouraging a diversity of values and perspectives without fear of discrimination? This book attempts to answer some of these questions, not with one-shot solutions, but with certain techniques and methods that organizations can use to bring about some clarity in creating their own cultures, checks and balances.

Along with the increasing number of women (and non-males) in workplaces, the advent of globalization in India in the early 1990s has resulted in a spate of unforeseen consequences and implications on the average workplace in India. Although organizations were clued in on globalization's implications from the point of view of economics and business, nobody had really thought of the social, cultural and political outcomes it would have. Nobody had prepared for large-scale conflicts arising from outsourcing of jobs from richer countries; and conversely, for 'brain drain' with huge portions of India's workforce moving abroad in search of more lucrative opportunities. In the same vein, nobody fully realized that large-scale migration of labour would result in different types of conflict, shaping immigration policies and international relations for decades to come.

We opine that one major reason for leaving these issues behind is because they are not seen as 'hard' issues, unlike economics or business. They are seen as issues merely related to human resource (HR) management, which still remains as one of the most underrated departments in any organization. In fact, a common complaint made by HR managers today in large corporates is that even though they go to business schools and obtain similar qualifications as, say, persons in sales and marketing teams, other departments persistently ask, 'What do HR people even do?' Their roles are still misunderstood and discounted, much like the roles of nurturers and caregivers in families.

In families, many of us would have seen characteristic gender politics at play between the roles of breadwinner and nurturer, where the former is valued far more than the latter. This can easily be extrapolated to the organizational context, where we see parallels between 'good of the family' and 'good of the organization' being bandied about, more often than not to the detriment of the 'softer' members of the family and organization, who do not play respected 'masculine' roles.

Indian society and Indian law, in particular, has never engaged meaningfully with these types of questions. Indian law engaged, for the first time, with sexual violence and sexual discrimination through the movement culminating in the drafting of the Vishakha Guidelines, motivated by sexual violence as a form of abuse of power. Even thereafter, awareness around sexual harassment, violence and discrimination has always arisen in the form of a scandal. We see patterns emerge, where accused persons turn around and claim that they have been targeted as persons of power. This usually follows with a debate on consent, with a 'he said, she said' situation arising. Following all of this, although there is a collective acknowledgement that sexual harassment does arise in the workplace, there is no consensus on how to deal with it.

The prevailing law, namely, the Sexual Harassment of Women at Workplace (Prevention, Prohibition and Redressal) Act, 2013, is explicit in terms of procedure, but heavily gendered in nature, which, at the outset can seem exclusionary. Further, it calls for 'preventive measures' without putting thought into how those can be formulated, and the domain of sexual harassment as such seems to be an unregulated one, with the Ministry of Corporate Affairs, the Ministry of Social Justice and Empowerment, and the Ministry of Women and Child Development all turning a blind eye, seemingly because they do not know how to deal with it.

We can see, time and again, that when there is an accusation of sexual harassment, questions of gender, sexuality, violence and identity are raised, and the ultimate role of bystanders is that of the judges. We can also see that after an accusation, the air is rife with resentment, not only that this kind of violence still happens, but also resentment by some that 'anything goes' in the form of sexual harassment.

In this background, it is safe to say that this book would not have happened if the #MeToo movement had not taken place with the intensity that it had, in India and globally. The #MeToo movement spearheaded public outcry about the criminal justice system in India not being 'enough' to deal with sexual harassment and women's safety. It raised questions on what safety, diversity and inclusion meant at workplaces, and what it would mean for diverse people to engage safely in workplaces. It also brought in the question of what 'professionalism' would mean and the irony surrounding the fact that one would have to become a 'non-person' to be considered professional in a workplace. This book looks at how professionalism has been interpreted in a corporate context, where people are encouraged to mute their emotions and deal with conflict through judgement. Professionalism in workplaces means to sanitize discourse and conversation, to 'de-gender' women and men, and to leave everyone vulnerable to the stereotype that women are always victims and men are always perpetrators.

This book tries to look at these diverse issues from different perspectives, to really try and look at sexual harassment as a product of different historical, sociocultural and corporate factors that permeate into workplaces. Although the authors acknowledge that the current system is largely deaf to victims' and survivors' narratives, this book does not focus solely on victim/survivor perspectives. The authors acknowledge that this book is not intended to be 'activist' in any way and wish to inform readers that the graphic and detailed nature of case studies and analyses may be triggering for some. The process of listening to each other, engaging with uncomfortable issues and bringing out case studies on sexual harassment, power dynamics and interpersonal relationships at work can be anxiety-provoking and difficult, and readers may experience some disturbance in this regard. Further, this book does not intend to trivialize or dilute survivors' narratives and experiences, but to open readers' minds to what can construe sexual harassment and how harassment can be determined. The authors have endeavoured to tackle these issues with the utmost sensitivity and consideration to the wide variety of readers' identities and perspectives and takes complete responsibility for any triggers or trauma experienced.

It is important to mention that the authors do not intend to provide 'solutions' for case studies mentioned in this book or to postulate on the 'correctness' of any of the reactions or outcomes. Further, the authors consciously avoid judgement of any of these stories but sometimes provide their views on gender, sexuality and different frameworks that organizations can use to look at these issues and deal with sexual harassment. All case studies are by genuine volunteers, with names of participants changed to protect their anonymity. Further, any analyses provided are the opinions of the authors, with influences from Mr Ashok Malhotra.[1] Some of the goals of this book are to encourage self-reflection by people working in corporate workplaces, uncover taboos around sexuality, power and hierarchy and to encourage conversations that will help define key issues of safety, inclusivity and organizational values. This book aims to help organizations go beyond the straitjacketed Prevention Of Sexual Harassment (POSH) programmes and training in organizations that are far too inadequate in dealing with a topic as nuanced and layered as it is.

[1] Ashok Malhotra, *Indian Managers and Organizations: Boons and Burdens* (New Delhi: Routledge India, 2018)

Acknowledgements

We thank SAGE for having given us the opportunity to write this book, which we hope we have done justice to.

We thank Ashok Malhotra and Sarbari Gomes for the numerous serious and casual conversations and *addas* and their work on gender and diversity from which we learnt a lot. We thank all our colleagues at Sumedhas, Academy for Human Context, with whom we co-learn about ourselves as individuals, systems and communities.

We thank *Sanjog* for having given us an opportunity to learn about how the intersectionality of gender, power and sexuality plays out in rural communities and marginal communities of our society as well as in the non-profit sector, in activist organizations.

We thank our clients at Change Mantras from whom we continue to learn about the organizational dynamics and leadership challenges in building cultures that are inclusive and diverse.

We thank Krithika Balu for editorial contributions. Her insights as a lawyer and her skills in research have been invaluable.

And lastly, this book would not have been possible without the support of Manisha Mathews, whose patience and trust in us encouraged us to find time for this labour of love.

1

EASY FLIRTING OR COERCIVE PERSUASION

Socialization

gender roles

flirting

sexualized persuasion

'You must mate before it's too late', Rajeev smirked, Malini broke into giggles.

Malini was lamenting about how her Spitz was a 'biter' who had spared no one in the house, including her, to Rajeev, Shreya and Amrit—her colleagues—at an office party. Rajeev was the team leader and the rest of them were in his team, but he was friendly and never asserted his authority in an hierarchical way—at least not in spaces where they socialized.

'How old is she?' asked Rajeev. 'Nine years', Malini replied. 'Has she been mated?' asked Shreya. 'No', said Malini, and that's when Rajeev quipped, 'You must mate before it's too late!' with a smirk, and the rest of them all laughed at the innuendo.

It's a business process outsourcing (BPO) firm with a young crowd, where everyone is in their 20s or early 30s. While the office has strong systems on timing, attendance and leave, to keep up with high-pressure assignments and a highly competitive market, the office culture is relaxed about dressing, 'lingo', use of expletives in casual conversation and humour. Ninety per cent of the employees on the floor space are single, and the rest are newly married. After shifts, colleagues hang out and friendships have fostered, dating is not rare amongst colleagues and on the rare occasion when messy breakups have interfered with professional roles and the workplace, the HR has told them strictly to keep their personal mess out of office.

It's been three years for Rajeev in the company. He had joined as a floor manager after having worked at another BPO for a year, and now he is a team leader. Malini joined as an executive six months ago and reports to Amrit. She likes her workplace—it's fun and hard work combined, where colleagues are also one's friends.

Rajeev found himself attracted to Malini from the first time he saw her. She appeared smart, confident, youthful and fun to be with. He always found himself trying to be funnier more often than not when she was around. She seemed to be cool with his moves, his 'non-vegetarian jokes' as he calls them, his silent and sometimes voiced appreciation of her, clothes, beauty and grace. Malini laughs at his wisecracks and seems to enjoy his attention. He has hung out with her, sometimes with Amrit and Shreya and a couple of times just by themselves over coffee. It was not a formal 'date', but he was planning to ask her out that weekend for a movie and dinner. He was sure that she would agree.

When he messaged her that night (on a Wednesday) suggesting that they could catch a newly released Ranbir-Alia Bhatt film that Friday, she asked who else was coming along and when Rajeev said that it would be just the two of them, she refused. Initially, she said something about having to stay at home because her cousins were visiting, but when Rajeev insisted on at least going out for a drink, she refused saying that she would not be too comfortable going out alone with him to a pub. He was baffled. He felt a little irritated because he thought that he had read signals of mutual interest from her and could not understand her refusal. He asked her what her discomfort was, and she said that she did not want to date anyone from her workplace. Rajeev heaved a sigh of relief because he was not personally rejected, and that it was only an issue of maintaining professional boundaries. That, he felt, he could handle and persuade her to change her mind. After all, if things got serious, one of them could always switch teams or floors.

So he did not let that conversation thread die down. 'Let's go for coffee tomorrow after the shift,' he suggested, and she agreed. Malini's refusal to go out alone with Rajeev for a film and dinner had less to do with her liking or not liking him, but more to do with drawing boundaries for herself with colleagues. She understood that many of her colleagues go on dates, and some of them may be casual or serious. Many of their relationships are sexual as well, casual or serious. And she does not hold any judgements over them. But for herself—a middle-class Maharashtrian girl with a reasonably liberal upbringing—she had decided to hold some boundaries for herself in her office, with her colleagues. She felt she could handle the balance between being friendly, casual and professional. Workplace romances are too complicated, she felt, and having just started at work, she did not want to allow anything that could be messy.

That conversation over coffee was stressful. Rajeev could not assure Malini enough that she was being too uptight and that she should go with the flow, trust him and herself enough to be able to handle whatever should grow between them. It sounded romantic, for sure. But his persuasiveness irritated Malini. She found him patronizing and stupid. 'If he believes in going with the flow, then why can't he also take my rejection of dates as a part of the flow?' she thought but withheld her irritation.

Persuasion and chase were fun for Rajeev. It was perhaps the first time for him, of having a six years younger girl being so decisive in her mind, and he was enjoying every moment of it. He was determined and not willing to give up, perhaps, somewhere down the line, it had become more than his attraction for Malini and challenge for him. He liked challenges. It was this determination and passion for winning challenges that made him succeed in climbing the ranks professionally, exploit his networks well and build his confidence in himself that if he really wanted something, he would get it.

Over the next few weeks, what began as mild irritation for Malini had now turned into feeling coerced. Rajeev did not make any explicit threats of any kind—about her rejection of his proposal for a stupid date impacting her professional standing with him—but she wasn't convinced about his ability to demarcate the two so clearly. Clearly, the man has problems with boundaries, she thought. She shared the situation with Shreya, but Shreya also was not convinced of her reasons for rejecting Rajeev's invitation for a dinner. 'He's a nice guy, *yaar*! And it's not like you have held these boundaries very tightly until now, you too have laughed at his sex-jokes and flirted with him. Just chill and trust him', Shreya told her.

GENDER, SOCIALIZATION AND ROLES

Wooing, pursuing and persuading are often seen as a mating ritual in patriarchal cultures. Men must take the lead in proposing to women, they must be the first to express their love and attraction to them; women may offer hints to the man when she is interested in him but wait for him to make the move—is a norm across cultures. While, in reality, many women may state their interest in getting married to their lovers. The symbolic gesture of the man going down on his knees to offer her a ring is an image sold globally even to today's youth and that carries with it imprints of psychosexual roles of men and women.

Even when a woman rejects a romantic proposal, a boy is meant to make every effort to impress her, convince her to change her mind—this is the message that boys in many cultures and countries, including India, grow up with. They get this message from love tales in literature, films and popular culture. Indian films are replete with many such stories, songs where the man wins the consent of his love interest through feats of what is projected as bravery, prowess and determination. We see the 'hero' fighting villains and saving the woman from being molested, slitting his wrist and writing notes to her in blood, stalking her and harassing her until she gives in. While some films may have depicted such behaviour as villainous and predatory, there are also many instances where it has been depicted as a 'mating ritual' wherein the woman concedes and 'falls in love with the hero' after being convinced of his worthiness and love for her. Notwithstanding the controversies over misogyny in *Kabir Singh*, the film's popularity with India's youth cutting across cities and villages, reveals that the needle on romance and masculinity across social and economic classes in India rests on a certain idiom of masculinity where Rajeev's refusal to respect Malini's refusal would be a virtue.

Malini and Rajeev's story is certainly not as extreme. Rajeev neither beats up the villains to rescue her nor does he slit his wrists to write her letters in blood. But he does enjoy the chase, his aggressive play for Malini's consent to date him. He may even be oblivious to what part of this experience is driven by his attraction to Malini, per se, and what part of it satisfies his masculinity—his sense of his own prowess. Rajeev's behaviour does not come across as odd or out of line to an onlooker like Shreya because, in her worldview, his persuasiveness is expected. Especially since she points out to Malini that Malini did not hold her boundaries very tightly and allowed for and participated in casual banter, laughing at sexual innuendoes and, therefore, implying that she must take some responsibility of sending mixed messages to Rajeev. Shreya's gaslighting of Malini is not borne out of a personal benefit; she has nothing to gain from the circumstances one way or another—but she insinuates about Malini that if she has, intentionally or otherwise, sent inviting 'signals' to Rajeev, she is now obligated to follow through that 'unstated promise'. It is quite likely that Shreya would have applied the same logic to herself and convinced herself to give in to Rajeev's demands had she been in Malini's place.

Rajeev's psychological universe—of the world of men and women—makes him blind to Malini's predicament. He does not understand her need for drawing boundaries between personal and work relationships. He is also seemingly unaware of the implications of him being higher over her in authority in the workplace in this situation and how that may make his persuasions even more forceful. On the other hand, he sees himself as a man who is uninhibited about pursuing and claiming his desires and dreams, and not just restricted to romantic or sexual relationships, but in every facet of life. His own childhood messages and socialization as a man has always encouraged and appreciated him for being a go-getter, stating his desires explicitly and persisting with them until achieved. As a heterosexual male, he does not see himself being cowed down by resistance. He reads Malini's resistance as being her fears and anxieties about propriety and preoccupation with 'things getting messy'.

The organization where they work does not interfere in people's personal lives and does not have any policy on people dating or getting sexually intimate with each other. What it does have a policy on is Prevention of Sexual Harassment wherein one party has aggressed upon another within the organization and abused power and authority to transgress, intimidate, coerce or force to gain sexual favours. However, sexual harassment policies in organizations and the law do not delve into prevention; even though they are coined as prevention policies. Defining acts of what would be considered abusive and constituting statutory bodies, like the internal complaints committee (ICC), focus on redressal and not prevention. Given the reality that people in an organization have a differential understanding on boundaries, they may not realize how hierarchical power often—even unintentionally—translates into perceived coercion; prevention would require a different approach to enable and empower people to communicate and manage boundaries more effectively.

SEXUALITY IN ORGANIZATIONS

Many BPOs are youth-driven organizations. The nature of work fits well with young people, in their 20s to mid-30s, dominating the workforce. The culture of such organizations is youth friendly which reflects in its culture, management style, administration and human resource (HR) policies. Abiding by the laws of the land, such organizations may have a policy in place to deal with sexual harassment, and some of them may even have an ICC, as it is meant to be. In this case, Malini was not aware of the committee or its members. Even if she was, as she explained, she was not sure whether this situation would qualify as sexual harassment as Rajeev had made no unwarranted sexual advances or indicated any threat to get her to agree to his demands.

How do organizations then deal with such cases? Is it something that an organization should even interfere in? How can an organization police or monitor relationships that may grow between colleagues, even in different ranks? And should it, even?

Many organizations prohibit dating and romantic relationships or even marriage between members in the same office. In fact, in such organizations, when two people from the same office get married, one of them has to resign or—if the company is large enough—they would be transferred to another division or vertical. The codes of behaviour between people, especially women and men, in such organizations are meant to be strictly formal. Proponents of such an approach argue that this explicit policy brings clarity to employees on expected behaviour and codes of conduct. It lessens ambiguity and reduces the risks of potential messiness.

There are many who believe that such prohibitions simply sweep things under the carpet and make sexual dynamics between people in the workplace more insidious. It leads to greater abuse of power, wherein attractions in the workplace are held in secrecy and get closeted, the taboo evokes thrill and is therefore, more attractive and makes the young people in junior ranks more vulnerable to abuse. They feel that what may be more useful is for the management and HR to create an awareness and dialogue amongst people on the intersectionality between sexuality, power and hierarchy in the workplace. Under the diversity and inclusion programme, organizations could aim at making people more conscious and aware of how sexuality gets played out in a work-system, how it intersects with hierarchy, power and authority. That dialogue and awareness would diffuse unstated tensions and empower a system and its members to build stronger interpersonal relationships, co-hold boundaries between the self and role in a workplace more effectively.

Imagine, if you were Rajeev's supervisor where such a situation came to your knowledge, but Malini lodged no complaints and was unwilling to report or discuss the matter with you or anyone, what would you do? Would you take it up with Rajeev or would you depend on your ability to work through his possible defensiveness, denial or even lack of awareness of how power and gender intersect in such a situation? If you are a manager in the HR department, your options may not include a specific intervention with Malini and Rajeev since neither of them has reported any matter, nor has there been a third-party reporting. But you would need to design a different intervention that does not lead to gossip and any direct implication on these two people in particular. You could speak to Malini to reassure her, accept her anxiety about the consequences of reporting; but eventually, you would have to plan an intervention which was generic and not pointed, but it would need to address the issue of office romance, boundaries and violations.

2

CRYING FOUL!

Mild transgressions

interpersonal issues

power imbalances

hostile personal environment

Radhika Mathur's relationship with her boss, Amit Khanna, was well known. Radhika had jumped from a rival company three years ago and had joined Amit's team. She was 24 at the time—passionate and ambitious, strong and wilful, with an appetite to learn, perform, take risks and leaps of faith and prove herself. In a matter of months, her eagerness to walk an extra mile brought her attention—both admiration and envy—from her peers and colleagues who had been longer in the organization than her. Many found her aggressive; some felt she was over-ambitious and insensitive to others. But for Amit, she was a breath of fresh air.

Youngsters of today, Amit feels, have a strong sense of entitlement, they are conscious of their own abilities, sometimes far exaggerated and untested. When he first met Radhika as an interviewer, he found her a good balance between confidence, clarity and assuredness on the one hand and a grounded perception of herself as someone who was new in the sector and had lot to learn, to know. He wondered if this eagerness to learn and acceptance of her own knowledge that she gathered from her formal education and her past experience being limited, is a façade. However, once she was recruited and joined the team, he found her willingness to be wrong and make mistakes, to being corrected and criticized for wrong decisions and choices, to be real. She was reasonably anchored in her self-esteem and did not get caught with passive aggression or reactivity when being taught through her mistakes or being offered critical feedback on her lack of team-management skills.

It also became fairly evident to everyone in the department that Radhika had now become Amit's favourite in the team. She was the eager-beaver, and he was the master who had found his muse, his protégé. He was considered to be a fair manager and not necessarily partial towards her but his comfort with Radhika and his growing dependence and reliance on her as a right-hand was evident. Their work would, therefore, include lunch meetings; she would readily offer to help out with tasks and roles that were not necessarily hers but ones she would take on to assist him. Amit was single then—separated from his wife with whom he also had a two-year-old child—and was going through a messy divorce. Radhika was single and focused on her work, and both of them would work through lunches and dinners, to 16-hours in a day, often including weekends. He was clearly her mentor who would give her opportunities over her peers. If there was gossip around their closeness with each other, it remained only in corridors and out-of-office spaces. Amit was a senior professional in the company, valued for his resourcefulness and held a lot of power with stakeholders, and no one would want to get into any conflict with him. So, they were also careful about what was being discussed in front of Radhika in casual or informal conversations.

Over three years, Radhika got promotions, still working with Amit in the same team until she moved to a lateral position (to Amit) in the company. The first cracks in their relationship started to appear to other people in the office in planning meetings, where Radhika would challenge or disagree with Amit and propose ideas that he did not agree with. The tensions between them grew over time until their disagreements in meeting spaces turned into spats, almost personal. They would no longer hang out with each other, and projects that included both of them to work in the same team became fraught with interpersonal dynamics. Their conflicts had been, on occasion, escalated to the stakeholders, and it became difficult to discern the source of their growing mistrust towards each other.

Matters came to a head when Radhika filed a formal complaint with the ICC that she had been subject to sexual harassment by Amit, two years ago, when she was working under him. In her complaint, she referred to at least three incidents and events wherein Amit had allegedly proposed sexual intimacy and where, on each of those occasions, she had refused to him. These were out-of-office settings where the two of them may have been engaged in a professional task, within the city, and on one instance during an official tour. When Amit was informed about the complaint, he became livid. In his account, he retorted that the allegations were false, motivated to malign his reputation and credibility. While he did admit that in the first two years of their working with each other, they had grown close as colleagues and then friends, the incidents referred to in her complaint had a certain context to them. There were conversations between the two of them about how they had grown to trust each other, how close they had become and how Amit—who was going through a stressful personal relationship—had experienced Radhika as being supportive and helpful beyond their professional relationship.

In turn, Radhika too, disclosed several times to Amit about how she trusted and looked up to him for guidance, support, care and protection and attributed much of her own ability to learn and grow because of him and how she had idealized him as a man who was caring, sensitive and generous to a fault. The attraction was mutual, which also turned sexual and would have matured, in his opinion, to something more meaningful if she had not been further promoted to a lateral position where she now believed that she needed to individuate herself from him, compete with him to come on her own as an equal.

The members of the ICC investigated the matter and heard Radhika's complaints, with evidence of the incidents, the time, the situation and questioned Amit to determine the exactness of the events.

Incident no. 1: Radhika and Amit were on an international tour to meet with investors and clients, for business development. On a certain evening in Paris, they finished their meeting early in the evening and had made plans to go out clubbing. Both of them had had their drinks and Amit was high but not out of control. Conversations moved from work to life, love and dreams and, Amit, while speaking about his sadness over his strained marriage, spoke about his loneliness and how he realizes that his professional work, which used to be about adventure and learning, had also become his psychological refuge that brought psychological and emotional stability, routine and safety and predictability. He held Radhika's hand expressing his affection and gratitude and acknowledgement of how much he had grown to depend on her, and how important she had become in that journey. While returning to their hotel, he kept holding her hand, and Radhika did not recoil or refuse. When they had reached the hotel and Radhika reached her room—both of them were on the same floor with adjoining rooms—Amit stopped at her door and looked at her and asked, 'Would you like me to come in for a nightcap?' Radhika said (to the ICC members) that she did not know how to react; while she did sense his vulnerability, she felt uncomfortable—she was not attracted to him and did not want to have sex with him or have a relationship with him. She told him that she had to get on a call with her mother, and he looked at her and without saying anything, walked to his room.

Incident no. 2: After working late in the evening, Amit offered to drop Radhika home, which was not a detour from his route. This was not unusual, but on that day, while they were driving back, Amit insisted that they should go out for dinner. Radhika said that she was tired and wanted to skip dinner and Amit argued that skipping meals is unhealthy and that going for a drink and dinner would help them relax and unclog their minds, that unfreezing of an overworked mind is essential for creativity and thinking out of the box. Reluctantly, Radhika agreed, and after dinner, when they were returning home, Amit suggested that Radhika could come back to his place and stay the night so that they can start the day early together instead of having to spend time commuting. He said this smilingly, and Radhika tactfully declined and laughed it off, pretending to receive it as a joke and no more. But internally, she had received it as nothing short of a proposition.

Incident no. 3: While on a trip back from the UK, they had a stopover in Dubai, and they had missed the connecting flight. The airline had offered them rooms in a hotel which was far from the airport because there were no two rooms in the same hotel available. Amit looked at Radhika and said, 'I don't have objection sharing rooms with you; rather, I would even like it.' Radhika looked at him and without responding to him, told the airline staff that two single rooms would be necessary wherever available.

In their interview, ICC members found it difficult to arrive at a conclusion of a sexual harassment charge. Their argument pivoted on a single question—why did Radhika not file a complaint at the time when these incidents took place? Why did she wait for this long? Radhika, in her defence, argued that the incidents in isolation were, in her mind, mild transgressions based on assumptions, insistence of a certain kind that did not seem serious at that time. But later, as she moved up in her rank in the organization and, as an equal in rank as Amit, asserted her views, opinions and positions, she found his attitude towards her as a patronizing, patriarchal man who believes women to be as dutiful followers, even if they may be talented and confident, must be obedient and subservient to men. She started recalling many other moments, at the time, which were telltale signs and, in retrospect, these sexual overtures seemed not to be innocent and seeking intimacy like that of a vulnerable man but to lay a certain claim over a woman on whom he would bestow his graces upon, to surrender. It is not so much for herself that she decided to file this complaint but because she believes that not calling out transgressions allows for a certain culture to foster and impunity to go unchallenged. In their internal deliberations, the ICC members argued about how can the ICC arrive at a conclusion that believes these arguments over a counterargument of professional victimization?

The dismissal of the sexual harassment charges did not surprise Radhika but enraged her. If she is not trusted, despite having proven her loyalty and her trustworthiness to the company, then what chances did young professionals have in the company to receive justice, safety and protection in their workplace? She demanded that the board of directors cannot absolve their responsibility towards creating systemic safety and protection for women by arguing legal compliance alone, but also by engaging with concerns around boundaries, propriety and hygiene in the system. Without a commitment to that, diversity and inclusion programmes are nothing but lip service.

'I don't find vindication in this dismissal of the charge. I only find impunity of aggression and licentiousness wherein women can claim victimhood without being questioned, and any questioning on that is counter-accused as gaslighting.'

NORMS AND BOUNDARIES IN AN ORGANIZATION

Where does one draw the line between individual issues and systemic issues in an organization? For many people, Amit and Radhika's issues are interpersonal and do not belong to the organization. Many would argue that they are adults who are capable of handling their personal matters or matters of personal nature, such as attraction and rejection of propositions, and organizations should not have to interfere or monitor what goes on between two people. Amit did not force himself on Radhika, there was no coercion or assault involved in those situations and therefore, what Radhika construes as sexual harassment is a stretch. The fact that she reports the matter, claims that she did not even realize at the time and brings it up at a point when things went sour between the two on professional matters, suggests more of a power struggle. Some people would resent her for playing the victim card to suit her convenience.

On the other hand, a counterargument would raise questions about propriety and boundaries between people, especially of different ranks where one has power and influence over the other. If someone is in a position of seniority by rank, the significance of what this person offers to a subordinate is coloured by this rank difference. The rank difference, especially in a direct boss-supervisee relationship, makes the relationship more vulnerable to seduction, abuse of power, manipulation and assumptions of intent. So some would argue that it is not appropriate for officers in rank to proposition their juniors and such propositions are not personal matters and have an impact on the organizational culture and its boundaries. The argument will say that a younger or a new person in the organization may look up to their seniors and may be vulnerable to approval, the need to be liked, needs of being cherished, celebrated and feeling special; and such a person can be manipulated to transgress boundaries, which at a later point of time invoke guilt, shame, anger and a sense of betrayal. The intent of the accused becomes secondary to the experience of the accuser.

None of these situations, therefore, can have a simple and clear line of what is the solution and what rules must an organization apply. While there may be some broad norms that the system may generate for itself on boundaries and norms, values and cultures and how the organization would like to promote safety and dignity for its employees, at a superficial level, teams often come up with boundaries that aim at sanitizing the system, draw norms and rules that are tight and infantilize the perceived vulnerable, project symbols of purity and innocence onto women and symbols of aggression onto men. And such a process invariably pushes issues of gender and sexuality in systems under the carpet, thereby generating toxicity. There is no denying that while working together, human beings will seek safety and trust where they can be vulnerable, and this will involve attractions. It is for the system to engage with issues rather than deny them or wish them away.

We are in a stage of transitional patriarchy wherein we are moving from societiy with very clearly defined and divided social and work roles between men and women to a society where these previously tightly held divides between men and women's social and work roles are getting diffused. Therefore, we are in a process of re-exploring what masculinity and femininity would mean if not demarcated through a gender-based division of labour. We are struggling to deal with differential notions of honour, dignity and respect that we associate with men and women. For example, sexual humour in 'boys' spaces' become ways of male bonding while making a sexual joke from a man to a woman may be offensive. POSH addresses sexual harassment of women by men but does not consider the reverse or even sexual harassment of men by men or women by women. So what may be considered offensive for a woman may not be perceived to be applicable to a man.

To build a space that is alive to these issues and build safety, one would have to engage with questions such as:

1. What is the significance of one's gender in an organization? How does gender impact interpersonal communication, boundaries and trust?
2. How do people experience their gender distinctiveness in the system? What are some of the anxieties that people experience pertaining to gender dynamics and sexuality?
3. How do power, rank and gender intersect in an organization? How does this manifest in terms of dynamics, decisions, gain and loss?

These questions, though conceptual, abstract and theoretical, need to be worked through with people at all levels in an organization in participatory ways and enlivened through people's lived experiences. Collective exploration by a significant group in such processes, especially including senior management, helps uncap certain trapped energies in an organization that are taboo. Normally, people in an organization would not discuss how women and men have differential ideas about honour and shame with respect to their bodies and sexuality. Often, one observes in cases that a woman may report sexual harassment or abuse much later than when it takes place. Many such women often speak about how they may have experienced fear—of consequences of disclosure, not only in the workplace but also in the family, of guilt—'Have I said or done something to have warranted this, should I have said or done something differently?' of shame—of one's sexuality, especially for people who are very private about their sexuality or of anger—often towards oneself or others. Often, this delayed reporting also triggers doubts and suspicions about the woman's integrity, intent and motives. The reality is that issues of sexuality are considered very personal and private in most societies and communities, and women and men grow up with some distinctive experiences and values around their sexuality. So if an organization needs to create an enabling environment where people would feel safe, confident and not be caught in guilt or shame in talking about transgression or violation, it would necessarily need to create a culture that enables people to talk about sexuality. And this is not easy; it is not an issue of a one-time training at the time of induction. It requires a designed intervention in the system to build that preparedness.

Amit and Radhika's conflict was layered. The issue, prima facie, was an interpersonal conflict stemming from professional differences, power struggle, feelings of betrayal and mistrust. The ICC found Amit's propositions to Radhika inappropriate but also found no clue of any adverse reaction from Amit when Radhika refused to have a sexual relationship with him. At the time of registering the complaint, Radhika had said, 'There are many ways men may patronize and subjugate women in an organization, and if those incidents were to be read in isolation, you would never find a case for sexual harassment. I find the assumption that the only way men may be seen to oppress or harass women must be sexual very limiting.'

It is critical, therefore, for management of an organization to build preparedness in the system to be more aware of gender dynamics and how paternalism may trigger rage conflict and power struggles between men and women in their workplace.

3

THE WHISTLE BLOWER

nterpersonal dynamics

veiled propositions

sexual favours

consent

Aanya Banerjee was excited about her new job. She always wanted to join an organization that works on social change and find a job that would be meaningful. After having worked in the banking sector as an HR professional for nearly 16 years, she started to explore and look for options in non-profit organizations. It was at this point that she came across an opportunity in an international charity organization that worked on the eradication of hunger and increasing food security of people. The position was of a deputy director for the country office in India who would be looking at HR management and the learning and development (L&D) portfolio.

Aanya's boss, Mr Dipankar Sanyal, a stout man in his 50s, was a jovial and charming man. When she first met him in her final round of interview, she found him to be warm and forthcoming, a sort of person one feels comfortable with without much effort. He put her at ease, and the interview was more of a conversation with her asking him more questions about the organization and the sector than him questioning her about her experience or credentials. 'Your questions, your curiosity and your interest in the social sector were your biggest qualifications for the job, as far as I was concerned. With your professional experience, I had little doubts about your ability to take on the challenges of managing people and systems in this organization. And your inexperience in this sector would be more of an asset than a disqualification, I felt', he later told Aanya shortly after she had joined the organization.

Dipankar seemed to be popular amongst the staff and had been the CEO of the India office for over a decade. Most of the staff in his office were recruited by him, and he enjoyed their loyalty. He knew everyone by their first names and seemed to know about their family situations quite intimately. They affectionately called him DS, and he called everyone else by their first names. The office had 39 people on the payroll with 18 programme managers whose job required them to visit the field projects every month across India, 6 people in finance, 3 people in the HR department, 2 in procurement and logistics, 1 administrator, 3 secretaries and 6 support staff including drivers and cleaners for the office. It was a moderately sized office for a national programme of an international organization that was headquartered in the UK. The team was diverse in terms of its gender composition, with more women than men, the programme managers were professionally qualified and the administrative staff having worked for several years. Attrition was low in the organization, and loyalty seemed to be high.

Dipankar often accompanied the programme managers on field trips, at least once a month. These trips would be to various parts of India and given that the project sites were often in rural locations, accommodations were arranged in hotels, guest houses and circuit houses, whatever was available at close proximity to the projects. In her initial months after joining the office, Aanya would often accompany the programme managers during their monitoring visits to acquaint herself with the ecosystem, projects and its implementing organizations. She enjoyed these visits immensely. It offered her opportunities to learn about India and its culture, its people and diverse communities and their cultural and social practices much more than she had ever learnt through her reading and previous professional exposure. Back in the office, she would have long conversations with Dipankar to understand his vision for the organization, the team and the programmes. She found him to be a good balance between being stable, often conservative in his risk-taking, and dynamic at the same time, wanting to come up with projects that were innovative and impact-driven at the same time. India's biggest challenge was to reach its stocks of grains from storage to communities and people who were malnourished, children who were stunted due to poor diets and lack of nutrition and unless the problem was addressed through a multi-pronged programme of empowering people to demand better governance, addressing social and structural problems that created bottlenecks between demand and supply and the vision of the country leveraging on its young population would remain unachieved. With each passing day at work, Aanya's satisfaction from her job grew and she felt proud to be part of a transformational movement in the country knowing her work had an impact on the fortune and well-being of hundreds of thousands of marginalized people in the country, children in particular.

A few weeks later, Aanya was scheduled to visit a project in Assam with Deepti, one of the senior programme managers, who was monitoring the project. However, due to a family crisis, Deepti had to withdraw from the trip and proposed postponing the visit by a month. Dipankar stepped in and suggested that instead of postponing the trip, he would go for the project visit, and since he had not visited the project for over a year, it would be helpful for him as well. Aanya was looking forward to the visit as well, and she felt that it would be interesting to accompany Dipankar since she would get his perspective on the initiative.

From Guwahati, they travelled to Kokrajhar district by car, which took them about four and a half hours. As is the practice, rooms should have been booked at the circuit house in the town. Upon reaching the circuit house, as they tried to check in, they were told that a twin sharing room had been booked for them. Aanya was shocked as she realized that since the original plan was for Deepti and her to come together, the office had booked a twin room for them because the circuit house was fully occupied and two single rooms were not available. However, the situation now was quite different, and while she was checking hotels they could find rooms, she was horrified to hear Dipankar suggest that they should consider taking the twin room, now that they were there instead of wasting time trying to find another hotel. She was so surprised that she started stuttering, wondering how he could have even suggested such a solution. It took her a few minutes to find her tongue and tell Dipankar, 'I don't think that sharing rooms is even an option for me. If you are feeling too tired to look for rooms in another hotel, I shall take the car and look for one as close to this house as possible.' Dipankar immediately retorted, 'Of course, of course. I am not tired at all, let's go look for another hotel where we can find accommodation. I was only suggesting the option of sharing rooms because we are so familiar and comfortable with each other and I certainly would not feel uncomfortable. But I completely understand your need for separate rooms, let's go!' Aanya didn't like the way Dipankar made it sound as if her insistence on separate rooms was uncompromising, but at this point, she chose not to say anything. They loaded their bags in the car and after searching for four other hotels in the small town, chose one which seemed clean and had two rooms to offer.

It was 5.30 in the evening by the time they checked in. Dipankar called Aanya in the room to ask her if she was comfortable in her room and suggested that they meet at 7 PM for dinner. Lying in her bed, without having changed her clothes, Aanya felt strange. She wasn't sure how she would interpret what had happened—Was Dipankar trying to proposition her? She tried to recall if, in the last so many weeks that she had interacted with him, there were any suggestions from him to her that she had missed. Should she just consider it insensitivity and stupidity of a grown man or should she feel offended? Was she being too prudish, or was she right in her reading more in the subtext of this seemingly trivial matter than was due? As she started replaying the moments in her mind, she was reminded of so many incidents in her life from her childhood, adolescence and youth when she had felt exactly this way. A private tutor making a comment about her hair, an older cousin who had the habit of putting his arm and fingers around her shoulder and grazing her budding breasts, a man holding her waist as he was making his way out of a crowded bus or a colleague she met at a conference getting drunk and insisting that they should play strip poker for fun—What was common in all of these moments is her dilemma of not really being sure of the intent of the other person and being in doubt of her own feelings and what of it was legitimate or not. She felt anger welling up in her, anger at herself and anger at her doubts. This doubt niggled at her, never allowed her to take a stance, neither did it allow her to express her feelings, lest it was wrong and misplaced, nor did it permit her to do away with the memory of how she felt in those fleeing and temporary moments. The gaze, the grazing hand, the leering words or the drunken proposition may have long gone, but she felt like a captive of doubt asking herself, 'Did it really happen?'

With all of these thoughts running in her head, she may have dozed off, only to be awakened by her phone ringing.

It was 7.45 PM, and she heard Dipankar asking her if she was ready for dinner. For a minute, she felt blank and mumbled something about coming in five minutes. Much as she wanted to remain curled up in bed and sleep, she had always been respectful of professional etiquette, so she made herself freshen up, change and prepare for a cordial interface.

The hotel was an old house restored and renovated. It may have belonged to the managers of a tea estate, but now with the dwindling state of the tea gardens, the estates have either converted these properties to hotels or sold them off to hoteliers. The dining room was a large hall on the ground floor and next to it was a large veranda which opened into a thick green patch and a view of hills at a distance. The veranda had cosy cane garden chairs and tables, painted bright green. Dipankar suggested that they sit in the veranda. The waiter brought the menu, and they ordered dishes that were prepared in the local Assamese way, which was not too different from the Bengali taste. With some effort from Aanya, conversation flowed easily about their past associations with Assam, the social context and politics of the state of which Dipankar seemed to know a lot, anecdotes of dealing with corrupt politicians and dealing with the mafia, and by the end of the evening, Aanya felt a lot calmer. If Dipankar sensed the stiffness that she felt in her, he certainly did not show it.

The rest of the trip was uneventful in any unpleasant way. It was engaging and absorbing for Aanya, and she again got to see Dipankar at work, which was sharp, insightful and deft, and it was a delight to watch and learn from him. Each day, they would leave the hotel at 9.30 AM. Dipankar suggested that they should meet at the veranda for breakfast at 8.30 AM, and even though Aanya was not used to having anything more than a cup of coffee in the mornings, which she ordered to her room, she believed that joining colleagues for meals was a mark of respect. And the conversation with Dipankar was never a problem. On the third and last day of their visit, when they were lounging in the veranda, Dipankar said he felt like having a drink and asked Aanya if she would like to have one. Aanya refused for herself but assured that she had no problem if Dipankar chose to have a drink. As they spoke about the project and what they had learnt and observed, Dipankar asked Aanya what she thought of him. She paused for a minute and asked him, a little nervously, what he meant by the question—Was he seeking her opinion of his professional skills, or her experience of him as a person? 'Well, whatever you have seen and observed and experienced me...', he said, which left a door so wide that it could lead to anywhere. Aanya gathered herself and chose to share with him her observations on how she saw him dealing with various stakeholders, his questioning skills which were less interrogatory and more exploratory, his ways of enabling stakeholders to share their unhappiness or complaints with the organization if any and how, in Aanya's experience, there is a distinctive flavour in the way he operates with people and how many of his programme managers deal with similar situations. She went on to speak about how she experiences his leadership, which came from personal passion towards the social cause, the ability to look at the larger picture and, therefore, pick and choose his battles, deploying diplomacy and tact to overcome stress in relationships and collaborations, and so on.

'Anything that you don't like about me...?' asked Dipankar. Aanya looked at him, square in the eyes, wondering if he was trying to provoke her. 'It's too early for me to form my criticisms of you', she asserted. He smiled, and they ate their meal in silence for the next five minutes.

Several months passed since then. After her experience in Assam, there was no opportunity for Aanya and Dipankar to travel together. Interfaces in the office were cordial, functional, professional and polite—the work that they enjoyed brought them together. Aanya was working on artefacts on leadership and partnership management for the organization based on the current practices of the senior managers and the CEO, which was an engaging and interesting exercise. It gave her plenty of opportunities to interact and engage with her colleagues, who were also curious to learn what emerges from her study on leadership in the organization, and how it impacts the organizational identity and culture, and hence its influence on external stakeholders.

Aarti Dasgupta was in her late 30s and working as a senior manager in the organization for over five years. She laughed easily—sometimes in genuine humour, sometimes to escape a difficult moment or embarrassment and sometimes simply out of habit. She was one of the managers Aanya was studying and learning from—on her management and leadership style, decision-making, underlying values and principles, beliefs and convictions, what she would compromise on and what she held sacrosanct, and how this reflects in her interfaces, role taking and how she shapes the organizational identity and culture, internally and externally. One conversation with Aarti led to a question on how she finds gender impacting role taking, efficiency, management and leadership styles and organizational culture. It was an extremely engaging conversation wherein she shared how a mostly woman management team with Dipankar as the benevolent patriarch mirrored a polygamic family in many ways. She giggled as she explained how the women managers in the firm would compete for affirmation and approval from the old man, which was natural in any system perhaps, but also where gender and sexuality play a role in it, wherein the male manager's relationship with their boss was distinctively different from some of the dynamics between the women and Mr Sanyal. Aarti stopped herself at this point and shied from naming or offering examples—she looked at Aanya and said, 'You must have observed, it is your job to have observed....'

Gender does play a role in interpersonal dynamics. How men and women engage with each other, how they behave with each other is a part of socialization and culture as much as their own primal makeup—their attractions, repulsions, fears or desires. We learn to deal with our feelings of attraction through the norms of appropriateness, and in a workplace, we learn to mask our attractions because that is what professionalism demands of us. However, these attractions may leak and manifest through flirtation and care and sometimes grows into something more when it may be mutual. It also leaks into exploitation when the attraction is not mutual and is laced with power dynamics in an organization. Aanya mulled over what Aarti had said and thought of how she had experienced gender impacting interpersonal relationships in the previous organizations. The thought made her more curious than vigilant, and she thought of taking the question of how gender impacted their role taking and organizational culture to other managers in her interaction with them.

The following month, Aarti and Aanya had decided to meet over coffee, out of office. Aanya had made a few friends in the organization, and Aarti was one of them. She liked Aarti—she was intelligent, passionate and carefree and also tactful and diplomatic. She loved the work she did and was diligent about it. At the same time, Aanya sometimes detected traces of anger or sadness in her conversations and expressions, but they were fleeting at best. She was a single mother who got divorced three years ago but seemed centred and settled in her own life. She was confident of herself, professionally and personally, and could deal with social challenges that single and divorced women go through in society, without much rancour. Being propositioned for casual sex was not uncommon, and for Aarti, a sexual proposition from a man whom she gets to know socially or through a dating website was not taboo. She had the power to decide what to respond to and how and knew well to ward off what was not welcome. Her confidence also, perhaps, prevented predators from taking risks with her.

'But not all women are in my situation. If you look at the three secretaries in our office, they are either single, divorced or have huge financial responsibilities in their families. Their professional qualifications are low, and if they were to lose their current jobs, they would have a difficult time finding another one in the same pay scale and with arrangements that suited their personal life situations and demands of caregiving to their children or parents or in-laws. That is what makes them vulnerable to compromises. They have all had affairs with Sanyal, one of them still has some kind of an arrangement I suspect, and she is married. These 'affairs' come with a payoff and at one level, it would seem that these affairs are wilful, consensual and by choice. But are they really?' wondered Aarti.

This disclosure disturbed Aanya. She disclosed her experience of Sanyal during their trip to Assam. Aarti did not seem surprised, she said, 'He threw you a bait, and you were strong enough not to fall for it. The bait may be a veiled proposition and had it only been with you, it may have been an accident. But when these incidents are with multiple women over a period of time, there is a pattern. Isolated, none of these incidents can establish a charge of sexual harassment and, therefore, no one person would ever take the risk of filing a complaint.'

Slowly but steadily, things were becoming clearer to Aanya. There was an ICC in place in the organization. Yet in the last 10 years, there has never been a complaint filed to the committee. The sexual harassment policy said nothing about codes of conduct regarding sexual relationships between people of different ranks within the organization. Neither did it say anything about sexual relationships between people of the organization and any of their stakeholders, for example, the partner implementing organizations who were fund grantees of this organization.

A year had passed since, and Aanya had all but set aside her doubts and questions regarding ethics, morality and sexuality that had triggered from her conversations with Aarti. Until one day, when she was in Sanyal's office and he had stepped out for a moment to take a call, they were trying to locate a document in his computer, and Aarti continued to search for the file, even after he had stepped out. As she searched the documents folder, she clicked on a folder in My Documents that opened to several intimate pictures of Sanyal and Shahana Basu, one of the secretaries. Aanya was shocked at what she saw. While she had heard about Shanana's affair with Sanyal, she was alarmed by the fact that these compromising pictures of Shahana were in the office computer which was, in her opinion, a complete violation of all professional ethics. Without a second thought, she mailed herself the folder without having decided what she would do with them. She deleted the item from the sent folder to avoid Sanyal detecting what she had done. She hurriedly left his room and went to her own desk, trembling with rage. She decided to give herself some time and decide on the action the following day.

What transpired next in that office was nothing short of melodrama. Aanya filed a complaint with the sexual harassment committee detailing her observations, own experience with Sanyal and what she had found in Sanyal's computer. Even though the sexual harassment policy requires the victim to be the complainant, in this case, she decided that the clause assumed equality of power between the accused and the complainant and, in this case, the issue was not just about whether Sanyal was guilty of sexually abusing Shahana but about his own abuse of power to get sexual favours. The ICC members met to review Aanya's complaint and decided to proceed with the investigation that would include intimating Sanyal about the complaint and seeking a response and interviewing Shahana to find out more about her relationship with Sanyal. The ICC could not agree on how to find out whether Sanyal had abused his powers with any other women in the office, the committee was bound by clauses of privacy of the investigation and unless and until someone came forward on their own to file a complaint, they had no powers to proactively inform others about the complaint and interview them, unless Sanyal or Shahana called them as witnesses. Matters got even more complicated when Aanya decided to keep the HR chief in the UK informed about this complaint because the accusation was towards the most powerful person in the country office and, therefore, the investigation was vulnerable to bias unless also monitored by the company headquarters. This disclosure resulted in a spin when the HR chief in UK informed the CEO of the headquarters , who also took it upon himself to 'unofficially' have a conversation with Sanyal, to get his response to the complaint.

The investigation led to three key findings. First, Shahana denied any charges of harassment or sexual abuse by Sanyal. After trying to deny any sexual relationship with Sanyal, when questioned about how Sanyal may have found her photographs in vulnerable situations, she admitted to having had a relationship in the past, and that was a personal matter, and the relationship was ended by the two of them, mutually. Following the interview, she later sent a letter to the committee complaining against Aanya accusing her of breaching privacy and stealing her pictures from Sanyal's computer, with whom she had shared those pictures willingly. Second, Sanyal admitted to the relationship and repeated the same version of it having been ended mutually, as Shahana had done. Third, the ICC responded to Aanya that while her questions on ethics may be valid, Sanyal cannot be accused of breach of the sexual harassment policy because there is no complaint from the so-called victim. Assuming responsibility on behalf of the victim would be infantilizing her authority to decide for herself. As far as the issue of sexual relationships between organizational staff goes between members of same or different ranks, it would be a stretch to assume that sexual relationships between members of different ranks are equivalent to abuse. The committee also could not arrive at any conclusion on Aanya's charge of sexual harassment over the Assam incident since there was no corroborative evidence and it had also been over a year since the incident happened, and there was no satisfactory explanation why Aanya had not filed a complaint earlier if she felt that she had been sexually harassed. The headquarters accepted the report.

Aanya resigned from her job the next day after the committee filed its report. Sanyal continued in his role for another year and then was promoted to the London office the following year.

This incident is a classic example of a system that takes the Prevention of Sexual Harassment law as a matter of statutory compliance and does not work with it. While the law speaks most specifically about redressal mechanisms, what an organization needs to do to prevent sexual harassment is glossed over. In this case study, Aanya's arguments raise three very important questions:

1. What is consent? How do we understand the issue of consent in a system? How do we understand coercion and vulnerability and abuse of power? What would be the boundaries between a personal matter in an office space or amongst colleagues and professional codes of conduct?
2. What should be the norms of behaviours in an organization around sexuality?
3. What measures should an organization take to detect predatory behaviours, which can escape the loopholes of a narrow investigation process?

Whether an organization will or will not allow any sexual relationships between its employees is a matter that most organizations engaging in this question have not been able to respond to, with clarity. Some organizations allow and even encourage marriage between members of their staff. Other organizations have rules of couples not working in the same departments. Some others have an unwritten understanding that bosses should not have any affairs with their subordinates. And few organizations, if any at all, seem to have found answers to how the ICC should deal with a report where the alleged victim may deny a claim of harassment, but there could be circumstantial data that speaks of predatory behaviour by a power holder in the organization.

4

BYSTANDERS' BETRAYAL

Office friendships

betrayals

bystanders

neutrality

One of the patterns in experiences of people who have reported sexual transgression and/or harassment at the workplace is the lack of support and abandonment from colleagues, including the ones who they thought were their friends. 'It was a rude shock for me when I realized that the people who I thought were my close friends refused to trust me and believe me when I shared my experience with them and sought their support. Today, I realized that these office friendships mean very little when it comes to having to take risks to stand by your colleagues and friends', says Razia, when she recalls a time she had been a victim of her boss's licentiousness.

Razia Fernandez looked at her friends in shock. Harleen, Amit and Reena avoided eye contact, looking down. Sahil looked back at her, defensively. 'Are you all serious?, Razia exploded. No response. Razia couldn't take it anymore. She got up and stormed out of the conference room, shocked, angry and disappointed.

Razia sat down in her office, dazed and furious. She took a few deep breaths, trying to calm herself down. As her anger dissipated, she found herself thinking about the past several months. As a mid-level advertising executive looking for her big break, Razia had joined the Alpha Advertising Agency about four years earlier and had immediately been floored by the energy, bustle and dynamism of the workplace. Alpha's founder, Vinod Malik, was something of a legend in the advertising business who had started the company from scratch in his 20s. Over the years, he had built his company into what was, now, one of Mumbai's busiest, most successful advertising agencies.

Like her friends, Razia had joined Alpha looking for a breath of fresh air and had thrived in the energetic environment. She had made a steady group of friends who socialized outside work regularly, and her colleagues, Harleen and Reena, were now her best friends. Professionally, she had never been in a better place. When she had joined the company, she had been listless and slightly lost, career-wise. Having the chance to work with Vinod Malik and his dynamic team had given her a whole new lease on life, and for the first time in years, she found herself driven, focused and actually excited about her work.

Razia leaned back on her desk and sighed. She thought about how and when she had initially joined the office, she had been quite intimidated by the idea of working for and with Vinod Malik. Although he was a trailblazer in his field and a genius in the world of advertising, she had heard rumours about his 'questionable' behaviour around female associates. She had dismissed those rumours in her mind, though, telling herself that people would always be jealous of others who were successful. Even when she had made friends and tentatively asked Harleen and Reena about the rumours she'd heard earlier, they had shrugged it off. He was an attractive older man, there were a lot of younger women in the office, hours were long and affairs between colleagues were commonplace. What more was there to it? Razia had also put those rumours out of her mind, telling herself that she was there to work, and that was it.

The rest, as they say, was history. Now, four years and three promotions later, Razia was sitting pretty in her corner office doing quite well for herself. She'd never been interested in getting married and had always maintained that she had no time for romance. Her friends' circle was tight, especially her office group, and she never felt the need for a companion or a partner, being fiercely independent and passionate about her career.

Until now, over the past few months, Razia had felt an increasing sense of desperation and urgency about the events at work and wished she had someone to talk to, whom she didn't work with and who would be an impartial and non-partisan listener. It had all begun about a year ago when she and Vinod were preparing to pitch an advertising campaign to a huge client. Being a high-stakes deal, she had thrown herself into work and had worked nights at the office for almost two months before she and Vinod flew to Gurgaon to make the final presentation. Vinod had worked almost every night with her too, ordering dinner and late-night snacks in the office as they worked into the wee hours, sometimes even greeting the sunrise before heading back to their homes.

Initially, Razia had been awed by Vinod's endless energy, the sharpness of his mind and his ability to extract ideas and concepts from her that she didn't even know she was capable of delivering. She told herself that this opportunity to work with Vinod directly was a huge learning experience and secretly felt flattered that he had chosen her to work with on such a high-profile client.

However, gradually, Razia found her feelings of admiration being slowly replaced with a growing sense of uneasiness around Vinod. She couldn't pinpoint it on one particular thing but on a number of things that he did or conveyed—from maintaining eye contact with her for just a few seconds too long, from his body language when they ate dinner together, or from him sharing bits and pieces about his personal life that she wasn't sure were appropriate. She began to dread their late nights and found herself unable to avoid them or make excuses to go home early, as their deadline for Gurgaon was fast-approaching.

She had first approached Reena for advice. 'What happened, love? What do you mean you are uncomfortable around him? Did he do something to you?' Reena had asked, brimming with concern. Razia found herself unable to respond properly. 'Well, he hasn't really done anything, per se', she found herself saying. 'It's more of my feeling that he's just a little too over-friendly and a little too interested in me', she had said, unable to provide any more details, even though Reena probed for a while trying to find out specifics of how Vinod had behaved inappropriately. The conversation had ended with Reena sympathetically advising Razia to go home and get some rest because stress could be a 'trigger'. Trigger for what?' Razia had wondered. 'Does she really think I am imagining things?'

After that, Razia had spent a couple of weeks more working with Vinod, questioning herself whether she had just been paranoid. However, as the days and weeks went by, she felt more and more uncomfortable around him noticing every glance he made at her when he didn't think she was looking, every single time he sat close to her or touched her arm while making a point and every instance of him bending over her shoulder to look at her work. She became a bundle of nerves, to the point where one day, Vinod told her to go home early because she seemed 'stressed out'. He called a car to take her home and then sent her a late dinner with a message to 'get some beauty sleep'. She found the whole thing quite disconcerting but struggled with herself from losing control and feeling reactive.

Things came to a head in Gurgaon. To everyone on the outside, it seemed like Vinod was the ideal boss—demanding but kind, attentive to his colleague's needs, charming and good-natured. To Razia, it felt like a living nightmare. She was the object of Vinod's undivided attention for the whole five days they were in Gurgaon, forced to spend the entire day with him and work nights with him at his suite at their hotel. On the first night they worked together, he invited her for a drink after their tasks were done, to which she refused. Another night, when it was pushing 5 AM, and she was falling asleep while they worked, he invited her to take a short nap on his bed, saying that he was happy to take the couch. She refused, aghast, and told him she would see him the next day and went back to her room immediately.

That incident was the final straw for Razia. After signing the deal and going back to Mumbai, she decided to file a sexual harassment complaint against Vinod before the organization's sexual harassment committee. Even though all details were to be kept completely confidential, she found whispers following her over the days following her complaint. Disconcerted, she decided to come clean to her friends and ask for their support.

'And so that's why I filed the complaint', Razia finished, looking around the table at her friends. They'd come out for drinks after work, as usual, and Razia had told them the entire story. 'I'm sorry, I didn't tell you guys earlier, but it was just so difficult for me to realize what was happening', she said. 'What do you guys think?' She looked around.

Razia was not prepared for the ensuing silence. Her friends looked at each other, looked down and didn't say a word. Finally, Reena said, 'I told these guys about the previous time you came to me. Are you sure you're not just overworked and stressed, Razia? You know how sometimes when we are under pressure, things may look more serious than they seem...', she trailed off. The others looked at Razia as well, some of them nodding. 'Yeah, girl. Are you sure you want to do this?' asked Harleen, concerned. 'Filing a complaint is a huge step, and he's the founder, Raz', she said. 'Yeah, Raz what about your job?' asked Sahil. 'What will you do then?'

Razia couldn't believe her ears. 'I can't believe you guys!' she burst out. 'I just tell you how I've been sexually harassed, and this is how you react? I thought friends were supposed to be supportive!' she said. 'Of course, we are your friends, Raz', cut in Reena. 'But come on, you have to think practically about this', she went on. 'Even if you say he sexually harassed you-'

Razia interrupted. 'What do you mean 'if'?' she asked. 'Do you not believe me?' She looked around at her friends incredulously, who looked uncomfortable. Reena replied quietly, 'See, it's not that we don't believe you. If you say you felt uneasy, we totally believe you, Razia. It's just that as your friends, we don't really think that Vinod did anything super inappropriate, which counts as proper sexual harassment'.

'Yeah, sorry Razia, we know it sounds bad, but you didn't have even one proper incident to talk about where he actually got 'sexual' with you', said Amit. 'You know these complaints are really serious, and they can end a man's career', he added.

'I don't want to speak for anyone else, but it's just difficult for me to understand how he actually harassed you', he said.

Razia looked at her friends in shock. 'Guys! He would make me work nights with him! He would make me stay in the office and his hotel room with him till sunrise! And what about him offering me his bed? Don't you find that really weird and inappropriate?' she said, desperately.

Harleen shrugged. 'At some point, many people have pulled all-nighters with him, Razia', she said. 'Sometimes work just calls for long hours, and it's how everything functions. You knew this when you joined', she pointed out.

'And honestly girl, you know Vinod', added Reena. 'There are so many rumours going around about him and someone or the other in the office, all the time', she said. 'Remember when Monica and he were working on that big deal in August? There were so many rumours going around and she got super upset that people were talking about her', she said. Everyone else nodded. 'But he didn't force you to do anything, and we all know you're not interested in him sexually or romantically', she said. 'Are you sure you want to go through this? Don't you think it's better to just move past this harassment complaint and just not add fuel to the rumours?'

'What rumours?' asked Razia. 'Come on *yaar*, of course, there are rumours going around about the two of you', said Amit. 'It was bound to happen since you both were working so closely together for so long', he said. 'Don't look so surprised, Razia! We ourselves have discussed and laughed over so many old rumours about Vinod and his various women', he said, with the others ruefully smiling and nodding their heads in agreement.

Amidst her whirlwind of emotions, Razia realized that Amit was right about this. Over the years, periodically rumours would surface about Vinod taking a 'special interest' in female colleagues, usually younger and attractive. They would work together closely, spend late nights in the office and would be the subject of gossip for a few months, after which rumours would die down till Vinod was linked with another female colleague. Razia and her friends had frequently talked about these rumours, usually dismissing them with a chuckle as idle gossip. In fact, Razia had opined to her friends that Monica, who Vinod had been linked to earlier, should have been more careful not to work so closely with him if she didn't want rumours being spread about her. 'We all know what kind of guy he is', she had quipped, laughingly. 'Of course, people will talk about him, and the only way to avoid the rumours is to avoid getting too close to him!'

Razia remembered her words with a jolt of shame. Little had she known that she would be in the same situation as Monica, less than a year later. She looked back at her friends and took a deep breath. 'Fine guys, I understand all your points', she said. 'But what I said earlier about Monica was wrong, and I should not have normalized Vinod's behaviour towards any of the other women', she continued. 'Don't you see that his behaviour crossed my boundaries?' she asked them. 'Isn't that itself wrong?'

'See Razia, it may be wrong in principle', said Amit. 'But you have to be practical. Do you realize that if you keep the complaint open, it'll become a huge scandal?' 'He's right, Razia', said Harleen. 'It's fine to idealize things and have strong principles, but what are you really going to get out of this?' she asked. 'Don't take this the wrong way but you're not married, Raz. If something bad happens, who will you lean on for support?'

Razia felt physically sick, hearing these words. 'Wow, guys', she said. 'I can't believe that you all, instead of supporting me, are tearing me down like this', she said. 'And why are you making it about me? What about you guys' role?' she said. 'Do I expect no support at all from you? I thought we were friends and that I could count on you!' she exclaimed tearfully.

Instead of a show of support, as Razia expected, her friends looked annoyed. 'Please, girl', said Reena. 'Be realistic. You know my situation; I have two kids to support and can't afford to be part of any scandal'. The others nodded. 'Yeah, Razia. We are here for you unofficially but you really can't expect us to be dragged into this', said Harleen. 'And for what? So that we can all be fired when the sexual harassment committee finds him innocent?' she said. The others looked accusingly at Radhika. 'Perhaps the best thing you could do is leave', said Amit, finally. 'Just put this behind you, put it behind all of us, and get a fresh start elsewhere', he said. 'You'll never be able to challenge the founder of this company and get away with it'.

The role of colleagues and bystanders in such situations is always tricky. They get torn between their loyalty towards their friends, their own judgement and stances on the situation, their concerns and anxieties with consequences of their involvement and loyalty towards the organization, the senior management and their relationship with the accused. In this case, Harleen, Amit and Reena were caught in their own dilemmas, which may have been different even if their collective stance was the same—not to get involved. Amit clearly chose to differentiate the inappropriate from harassment, whereas Reena seemed to insinuate that she may have been imagining the harassment and Harleen believes that men in power are likely to flex their privilege in different ways, and it was up to women to keep themselves in check. While Razia demanded their loyalty and for them to implicitly believe her and take sides against Vinod, her friends recused themselves from participating in any event of a sexual harassment complaint in fear of consequences on themselves.

It is a piece of common advice from mental health professionals that if a person discloses her or his experience of being sexually abused or harassed, he or she must be received, heard and trusted unconditionally. Does this mean and automatically imply that as a listener, you must automatically and implicitly accept that the accused is a perpetrator? Does trusting and believing in the complainant mean suspending all due process of investigation and proof before condemning the accused? Also, what happens if, as a third-party who was not present at the scene and I only receive and hear one side of the story, and in my judgement, I do not agree with the complainant? In this case, for example, in Razia's experience, the suggestions on sleeping in Vinod's room was inappropriate and corroborated with all other experiences of over-familiarity, suggestive remarks, transgressing time and space boundaries, it would tantamount to sexual harassment. Whereas for Amit, Harleen and Reena—there was a clear distinction to be made between what was inappropriate and when does it cross over to be labelled as harassment and unless the accused had directly propositioned or suggested sexual encounter with adverse implication upon refusal, calling it harassment would not only be inaccurate, Amit may have felt that it was unfair and inappropriate to level an accusation that was far exaggerated from reality.

What is interesting in the conversation is that it gets limited and restricted to arguments over opinions and beliefs and then turns emotional wherein Razia felt betrayed and accused her colleagues-cum-friends of betraying her trust. None of the three friends explored any questions with regard to how Razia felt at that moment or try to connect with her emotionally without getting caught in deciding whether those feelings were justified or not. Trusting or empathizing with a person making a disclosure is not about accepting their reality as your truth, it only means believing that this is how the person has experienced the reality and has felt about it. This may seem particularly confusing, so let's try and deconstruct this through a couple of examples. Your child comes from school and is distraught that his teacher in class humiliates and hates him. He narrates an incident from the day about how he had forgotten to complete an assignment that he was meant to and how the teacher humiliated him in front of the class but let go of others who had also not completed the assignment, and how he believes that his teacher hates him and looks for opportunities to victimize him. You could respond to this in three separate ways—first, focus on the physical data, evidence, corroborate with your son's classmates and then decide whether there is any truth in your son's complaint. The second approach could be to implicitly believe in what your son has said and register a complaint against the teacher or some such action to redress the injustice. The third may be to believe that your son felt humiliated and that he believes that he is being victimized, and how that has left him feeling sad, angry, afraid, anxious or however else he may have felt. Listening to him and validation of his feelings does not mean that you have to accept the facts he believes to be true as the only and whole truth and the only perspective in the situation. This is what empathy is—being able to connect and relate to someone's emotional state and not getting caught in trying to verify the objective reality. Razia's sense of betrayal comes from her experience of emotional desertion which, she believes, is a by-product of their mistrust of her and her friends not valuing or trusting her judgement or her experience.

The role of a bystander is most often projected as a judge. Bystanders are often accused of being selfish, driven by their self-protection, of colluding with the powers that are normalizing violation and violence and gaslighting the complainants, making them doubt themselves. Bystanders themselves often get caught in the role of a judge. Yet that is not the key task of bystanders. A bystander is required to be an empath, as in this case, where Razia needed to download how she felt during those five days, emotionally and psychologically, and what she had been through. That process would have helped to explore whether and how she may have felt about expressing her feelings to Vinod, what she may have found challenging and that conversation might have helped her consolidate herself emotionally and then decide on an action. Bystanders also need to have the awareness and skill of responding in situations of disclosure, and how, unconsciously, one may end up gaslighting the person disclosing the experience. These are skills that are not natural in most people, they are to be taught and learnt. Also, bystanders are likely to opine from their own beliefs and values on gender and sexuality, biases and stereotypes, therein. In this instance, Amit, while arguing against a sexual harassment suit for behaviours which he considers to be inappropriate, does not, therefore, state what, in his opinion, should be the actions against boundary transgressions or inappropriate behaviours. Reena and Harleen, and even Razia herself, had made light of the elderly boss's fixations with young, attractive women and had never raised concern about their own safety or the organizational culture and its normalization of the male privilege of a certain kind.

This case study touches upon a very common issue of accountability of people in positions of power. 'Is it worth it?' Razia's friends kept asking her—'be practical…'—revealing certain givens that they and many of us operate from—the reality of inequality of power between a founding member and a mid-ranking or junior employee, and in such power differentials, the person lower in rank will have to bear the adverse consequences of any conflict, no matter whose fault it is. Unfortunately, research on sexual harassment shows that such perceptions are not inaccurate and, therefore, despite constituting statutory compliance mechanisms and law on sexual harassment, in most countries the ratio between complaints and consequences tilt against the complainants and in favour of the accused.

5

WHAT IS ONE'S OWN BUSINESS, ANYWAY?

Bystander dilemma

personal v professional responsibility

bystander collusion

In fables and stories, we hear as children and, in later years, readers and the audience, when we find the villain of the story oppressing the vulnerable protagonist, our hearts go out to the hero and we find it very easy to take a stand and we choose to stand with the victim, the hero and against the oppressor. Yet in our living experience, we often find ourselves feeling abandoned when we find ourselves victims of injustice, and there is no one to support us, even if there could be 10 people around us, watching and listening. We believe that if no one else, one's family will always stand by us, our friends will stand by us. Yet in one's professional space, in the corporate world, people often have little faith in their colleagues taking a stand for the right—especially if it means that the opponent is in senior management, is powerful and influential in the organization. The simplistic explanation for this could be that bystanders are cowards and don't have the courage to take risks and stake their careers. In many cases, that could well be true. But sometimes, the dilemma of the bystander could be much more complex. It may have to do with the person's beliefs, values, one's definition of professionalism and even what one's role is in an organization and in shaping its culture.

Alisha was sending out some emails at her desk when her phone beeped loudly. She opened it to see a message from Neeta, 'Come down now urgent pls.' Surprised, she texted her back saying, 'What happened? Doing some urgent work', before continuing to send out the emails. Five minutes later, Neeta, out of breath and looking quite annoyed, showed up at her desk.

'Alisha, I messaged you', said Neeta in a low voice, so their colleagues nearby wouldn't overhear. 'Where were you?' 'Hey, I'm sorry Neeta, I have an urgent deadline, and Ramesh is breathing down my neck', said Alisha, not looking away from her screen. 'Shall we meet at lunch?' She looked up. 'Are you okay? You seem a little off today'. Neeta shook her head. 'I don't want to talk about it now', she said. 'I'm okay, but I want some privacy so that I can tell you what happened properly. I'll see you later', she said and with that cryptic remark, walked to the elevator.

Alisha was left wondering what Neeta wanted to talk about, but shortly thereafter, she became immersed in work and forgot all about it. Alisha was a mid-level employee in the procurement team of MRK, a successful international shipping business. She had joined the office about two years prior and was doing fairly well for herself. Like many employees at her age and level (Alisha was about 33 years old), Alisha's work mainly consisted of going to the office, sitting at her desk and not moving until her work was done and deadlines completed. She was a firm believer in keeping her head down and working hard, avoiding office gossip and all the 'distractions' as she called them, which came from being part of a large workplace.

However, Alisha couldn't avoid all office gossip. When she had joined MRK, she had met Neeta, who had joined the sales team at the same time. They hit it off at once and almost immediately became friends. Neeta was a more gregarious, outgoing individual who wasn't afraid to speak her mind at work. She had joined the sales team as a senior executive and was quickly and efficiently working her way towards a promotion. Office gossip was clear that three months down the line at appraisal time, Neeta was definitely being promoted to general management.

Neeta was Alisha's link to their other colleagues. Initially, when Alisha had joined the office, she had been a little awkward and shy, not talking to others outside the department. Neeta, however, had become quite popular in a short span of time and had encouraged Alisha to socialize with her and their other colleagues on a regular basis. Now, Alisha and Neeta both had a set of friends whom they regularly went out with after work, but their closest friendship was with each other.

After Alisha finished her work for the morning, she looked up at the clock and realized it was almost 1 PM. 'Oh no, I almost forgot I had to meet Neeta for lunch,' she thought to herself. She sent Neeta a text asking her to meet in the cafeteria and went downstairs. As Alisha walked up to the cafeteria, she saw Neeta waiting outside. 'Let's go get some tea?' asked Neeta, and they walked down the road to the tea stall together.

'What did you want to talk about?' asked Alisha, a little concerned because Neeta looked stressed out, fiddling with her phone. 'Is everything okay?' 'Well, I don't know', said Neeta. 'Something weird is happening. You know Rahul Mathew, right?' she asked, suddenly, 'The sales manager I've been reporting to for the past few months'. Alisha nodded. She knew of Rahul, a senior manager in his mid-40s, who had a reputation for being a nice person and a decent boss. He was rumoured to be ambitious, working long hours and pushing his team to go above and beyond their routine tasks.

'Rahul has been acting weird with me', said Neeta. When Alisha looked confused, she went on. 'Over the past few weeks, he's been paying a little too much attention to me', she said. 'I don't know how else to explain it. Earlier, I never noticed anything off or weird, but now, he's always asking me how I am, checking up on me, talking about work but also talking about unrelated topics and I don't know what to make of it.'

'Don't worry, Neeta', said Alisha. She felt relieved that this was what Neeta had wanted to share and that it wasn't anything worse. 'I'm sure he's just being a good boss. Now, don't get angry with me but has all your work been up to the mark?' she asked. Neeta just glared at her. 'Or maybe he's taking an interest in you because promotions are happening soon', said Alisha, hastily. 'He's probably just collecting information for your appraisal.'

Neeta shrugged. 'Maybe you're right', she said. 'But I've been feeling quite uncomfortable with the attention. You don't think it's inappropriate, right?' 'Not at all, Neeta', said Alisha. 'Don't give it a second thought. Now, let's go back in, we don't need our bosses noticing that we've disappeared at lunch!' They went back into the cafeteria.

Things went on as they usually did at MRK for Alisha, for the next few weeks. Everyone was working extra hard because of impending appraisals and bonuses and between all her deadlines, Alisha didn't get to see Neeta much, except for the occasional 'Hi' as they passed each other in the office. They didn't even get to eat lunch together, as Neeta seemed to be working overtime on a high-stakes project. One day, Alisha was sitting with their other friends at lunch when Savita, who worked in procurement, drew her aside. 'Did you hear about Neeta?' she asked. 'Hear what?' asked Alisha. Savita looked surprised. 'I thought you'd know', she said. 'Everyone's talking about it. Neeta and Rahul! Everyone's saying they're sleeping with each other.'

Alisha scoffed. 'Of course, it's not true', she said. 'He's married, come on!' Savita smiled. 'When has being married ever stopped anyone?' She walked away, leaving Alisha confused and a little irritated.

Alisha and Neeta arranged to meet that evening at a coffee shop after work. As soon as they sat down, Neeta started venting. 'I can't believe we haven't spoken in like two weeks', she said. 'You will not believe what has been going on with Rahul!' As they drank their coffee, Neeta filled Alisha in. Rahul, who had initially been giving Neeta a little too much attention, was now giving her small gifts and texting her every day. 'He actually messages me daily to ask if I have reached home safely', said Neeta. 'He's definitely interested in me, and I really don't know what to do', she continued. 'It's really awkward to have that equation with someone you're reporting to, and I really don't know what he wants.'

Alisha sighed. 'Honestly, I think you should let it go, Neeta', she said. 'You know how men can be temperamental. I think that you should just forget about all this and concentrate on work', she said. 'He's married, he's your boss and you really don't need this right now, especially with appraisals coming up.' She decided to not tell Neeta about the rumour she had heard from Savita, telling herself that Neeta really didn't need more stress. After they had their coffee, Alisha went home. As she was getting ready for bed, her phone rang, and she noticed that Neeta was calling. 'Why is she calling me so late?' she wondered.

Neeta was hysterical. After the first few moments where Alisha couldn't understand a word she was saying, Neeta calmed down a little and told Alisha what had happened. Apparently, after coffee, Neeta had gone back to the office to pick up some papers. She had bumped into Rahul who had asked her to have dinner with him sometime during the week. Aghast, she had refused and had told him she found his behaviour inappropriate, before walking out of the office.

'You won't believe what happened, Alisha', Neeta continued. 'I got home and just saw an email from Rahul that he sent 10 minutes ago, saying he wants me off this project! The email says that he's tried his best to work with me, made an extra effort to supervise my work, but he thinks that a different, *more competent* resource needs to be put on this project! Do you know how bad this makes me look?' she exclaimed. 'He's copied senior management, and I can just forget about getting promoted or a bonus or even being retained in this company, she finished miserably.

'I'm so sorry, Neeta', said Alisha. 'This is really ridiculous, and I can't believe this is happening to you! Why don't you try to get some sleep and just see if you can tackle this tomorrow at work?' she suggested. 'See if you can try talking to Rahul and sort this whole thing out', she said. 'Fine', said Neeta, 'Let me think about what to do.' They hung up.

The next morning, when Alisha arrived at her desk, the office was abuzz with gossip. Somehow, everyone had heard about the email that Rahul had sent, and everyone was speculating as to what had happened between him and Neeta. Alisha ignored everyone and sat at her desk. 'I should message Neeta to find out if everything's okay', she thought.

Later that day, Neeta suddenly came up to Alisha's desk. 'Come with me now', she said, urgently. 'I need to talk to you!' They went into the ladies' washroom, making sure it was empty. 'What happened?' asked Alisha, irritated. 'Is this drama really necessary, Neeta? I have a lot of work to do!'

'I filed a sexual harassment complaint against Rahul', said Neeta, abruptly. Ignoring the shocked expression on Alisha's face, she went on. 'It was bad enough that he was giving me so much attention, but when he sent that email, something in me just snapped', she said. 'I've worked so hard for this company for two whole years with no promotion, and he just tried to take that away from me with a single email. I can't just stand by and let it happen.'

Alisha could hardly believe her ears. 'I think this whole thing is such a bad idea. Why didn't you tell me before filing this complaint?!' she almost shouted. 'I thought you were going to talk to Rahul!' 'What's the point of talking to him?' rebutted Neeta. 'I told him I wasn't interested in him, and he immediately reacted by taking me off the project. It's clear that he's going to make sure I'm not recognized for my work, and I have to do something about it.'

'But it won't make a difference', said Alisha. 'Do you know what everyone's saying about you and Rahul? Someone told me a few weeks ago that you two were sleeping together. There are already rumours like that going around, so what's the point complaining? Anyway, it'll look like a lovers' spat gone wrong, so I'd say just drop it', she said. Neeta cut her off, mid-sentence. 'Alisha, I need your help', she said. 'Things have really escalated, and I need your support now more than ever to deal with this. Will you be willing to testify in front of the POSH committee that I was harassed?'

'Don't involve me in this, Neeta', said Alisha, noticing her friend's growing shock and disappointment. 'I just want to keep my head down and do my job. And I really don't know much about what happened. What will I tell the committee that you won't already tell them?' 'You can tell them what happened', retorted Neeta. 'You can tell them about our conversations and what I told you about Rahul's behaviour, and you can support me so that there's some evidence on my side!'

'This is really none of my business, Neeta', said Alisha. 'I only know what you told me, and I really don't want to get involved in this stuff. It'll just distract me from my work, and it won't even help your case', she said. 'What the hell do you mean it's not your business?' replied Neeta, outraged. 'How can you say it's not your business? It's bad enough that you just stood by while your colleague and friend got repeatedly sexually harassed, but now, you're refusing to help?'

Alisha felt helpless. 'It's not that I'm refusing to help', she said. 'I just think that this is between you and someone else, and I'm not involved', she continued. 'I don't want my name to be dragged into something that will just ruin my reputation unnecessarily. Just let me be neutral.' Neeta looked at her. 'Do you even believe me, Alisha?' she asked quietly. 'If you do believe me, if you do believe that I have actually been harassed—how can you, as my friend, as my colleague, take a neutral position? Or do you not believe me?'

This is Alisha's story. The story of a bystander, to an incident of sexual harassment in the workplace, who wanted to stay neutral. This story begs the question—can bystanders actually be neutral? Does the silence of bystanders count as 'neutrality', or is it just people being wantonly uninvolved with people around them?

Alisha's dilemma arises from her concern for her friend on one hand and her desire to stay 'professional' in the workplace on the other hand, without 'rocking the boat', so to speak. She firmly believes that it is not her responsibility to get involved in sexual harassment allegations and complaints, only feeling some conflict in this regard because Neeta is her friend, for whom she feels some amount of personal responsibility. It is interesting that speaking up does not form a part of what she feels is her 'professional responsibility' as part of a larger organization.

Underlying Alisha's reactions and thought processes lie perspectives and beliefs of organizations, membership of its people and the nature of the contract between an individual and the management. First, Alisha believes that the professional contract between her organization and herself is the role she holds, the tasks she is supposed to perform and results she is expected to deliver, her accountability towards her supervisor and ranks above and her being responsible in her job, taking initiative, being sincere in her work, etc. Anything else, to her, is a distraction and wasteful engagement, any 'non-work' engagement and socializing with other employees is gossip and waste. In her opinion minding one's own business is a great virtue and one's business is driven by the purpose of why the organization has hired her, articulated in her Terms of Reference. This is not Alisha's view alone, it is a view shared by many diligent, sincere and loyal employees in organizations across the world. Any conflict or crises is meant to be handled by the 'management', and the belief is perhaps that the organizational management is the responsibility of founders, CEOs and COOs, the board of directors or senior management. How does then upholding organizational values of the culture of safety and dignity, care, compassion and empathy, accountability and integrity play out is a discussion that she would never have engaged in or questioned. Or perhaps, those are read as behaviours that each person on their own must ensure and take responsibility for, but individual employees don't have any responsibility or collective participation and ownership of the culture they would create in the organizations. This is a classic case of self and systems fragmentation wherein the self is seen as an isolated island that has neither responsibility nor ownership of the culture which is collectively created, protected and nurtured. Such a philosophy is also encouraged and fostered in organizations by the top management. Collectivization has often been looked at with suspicion for fear of unionization, collective bargaining processes being abused by opportunists leading to harm to organizations and businesses. So espoused values articulated in the culture of the organization are maybe just a lip service, and values in action and practice could be quite different.

Second, Alisha's reaction and response to hearing gossip about Neeta's sexual liaison with her supervisor was instructive. Her decision to neither challenge it at the lunch table, nor share it with Neeta and later argue that in the face of such gossip of a sexual relationship, Neeta's sexual harassment complaint would be reduced to a lovers' spat and, therefore, the futility of escalating the matter speaks about how she may feel about being a woman. Here, she feels that if there is gossip or speculation about a male boss having a sexual relationship with a younger woman junior to him, the organization is likely to believe that to be so, even if the woman denies it. Further, if she then reports transgression, she would lose credibility in the organization and her report would not be taken seriously, and the matter will be dismissed and things will play out adversely for the woman. These speculations, when challenged, are often replied with 'this is life, this is what happens, I am just being practical...'—similar to what Amit said in the previous chapter. This further leads us to the question—If this is how she feels in the organization she works in, how safe does she feel, how fair does she believe her organization to be, how much integrity does she believe the system holds and how will all of these untested assumptions and beliefs play out in her interpersonal relationships with colleagues, how will it impact her ability to work in a team and how will this impact her creativity and psychological freedom in her workplace? Bystanders' silence, collusion, dilemmas in getting involved and taking stances (not necessarily out of loyalty or friendship but as someone who supports the organization in strengthening virtues of safety, transparency and integrity) speak about the nature of their membership of the system and, eventually, about the culture of the organization as well.

Cases like Alisha's, when reported to the ICC, often get dismissed or are declared inconclusive for lack of evidence; leaving the complainant feeling shamed, blamed and re-victimized. Complainants who fail to establish their complaints leave them feeling that they are now perceived as liars, who fabricated allegations for ulterior purposes, women who play the victim card for benefits and advancement. This stigma may be experienced—where the person actually hears comments from some colleagues, or perceived—the person may not have actually heard or been told anything but believes that this is how people must be thinking about her. The limitation of the way ICCs function today is that its job is only to determine the validity of a complaint against the accused and therefore, reach a verdict in favour or opposition to the complainant. It does not have an approach to understand the complex dynamics often involved in such cases and often it does not have the expertise to work with it to actualize values of empathy, fairness, integrity or honesty that it may hold in organizational vision and mission statements. Each such experience corrodes people's faith, trust and sense of belonging in the system; it may, however, strengthen beliefs that the organization belongs to the powerful, it is unfair to people in lower rungs of power and so on. Therefore, it is critical that organizations don't focus only on a reactive mechanism to deal with conflicts on issues of gender and sexuality and that it builds a holistic plan integrated with its organizational development plan. Experiential workshops and labs are helpful in building a culture that is not fragmented but nourished by the members collectively.

6

SOFT TARGETS?

Socialization; gender roles; flirting, sexualized persuasion

Abuse of power

sexual harassment complaints

male entitlement

generation gap

One of the refrains one often hears from people who have been accused of sexual harassment is that they were soft or easy targets. Many men, in particular, have often reported that they believed that they had been slapped with a charge because they were famous, wealthy and powerful and easy targets for slander, gossip and suspicion. A film actor who had been slapped with a sexual harassment charge by a younger co-actor had said,

> It's like the higher one reaches, the more envy one earns, and society enjoys vicarious pleasure by seeing someone fall from the heights. We are often coerced to cough up large amounts of money to get settlements out of court, to protect ourselves from the ignominy and disrepute. Often for people like us, who have spent lifetimes earning the goodwill, fame and success, it takes less than a lawsuit to suddenly feel and heat and lose face. In such matters, no one waits for the judgement, news reporters go to town with the report of the accusation, and judgements are passed on social media.

The accused claiming to be the victim of the wrong accusation and feeling victimized is a phenomenon fairly common in a number of cases where the accused is usually well known, has a lot hanging on reputation and is financially and professionally an achiever. Harvey Weinstein, Bill Clinton, Michael

Jackson or Tiger Woods, all had claimed at some point or another that they were being framed and that the motivations of the accusers were driven by greed for money and instant fame. And there may be cases where, in fact, accusations of sexual misconduct, transgressions and harassment may have been fabricated for motivations of compensation or otherwise. But often, the feeling of being victimized by an accused may stem from the belief that 'My actions were no different from others, but I have been pulled up and not others, because I am wealthy, powerful and famous, and therefore, the soft target.'

Mr Atul Menezes sat before two lawyers and wondered, for the umpteenth time, how he had wound up in this situation. As a well-known and well-respected entrepreneur in the Bangalore start-up space, he was used to many different types of attention—just not the kind he was receiving now. As an ambitious young man, Atul had left his hometown of Mangalore in 1995 to start his own tech company in the city of Bangalore. His intellect, never-say-die attitude and easy charm had not only made him a success in the Bangalore tech-start-up world but it had also brought with it a slew of young and equally ambitious individuals who had applied to work with him. After almost 25 years, he could look at his company and proudly say that not only had he created a venture that was highly profitable but he had also created a community of sorts, with a highly enviable work culture and easy camaraderie.

'So tell us what we can do for you, Mr Menezes.' Atul snapped out of his reverie to find the lawyers looking at him, waiting for him to tell them about his problem. He hesitated for a minute and then, with a deep breath, decided to dive right into the events. What was the point in beating around the bush about it?

'I am the founder and CEO of ZenTech Private Limited, based right here in Bangalore. I have recently been accused of sexual harassment by two female employees, and I am here because I need help to prepare a defence', he hurriedly said. The lawyers' expressions remained unchanged. One of them, a young lady, nodded and said, 'Tell us your version of the events. What exactly happened?' Atul hesitated again, wondering where to begin, and then decided again to dive right in and just answer the question from his own perspective.

'My sales and marketing team had brought in a big client whom we had been pitching our products to for months, about three weeks ago', he began. 'After the deal was signed, as usual, the entire team went out to a bar for celebratory drinks and dinner.' 'We do that quite often', he added. 'We go out together about once a month with the entire office and whenever there is something to celebrate. It keeps morale high and encourages team bonding outside a professional setting', Atul clarified.

'Anyway, at this gathering, I was sitting with a group of people from the marketing team, including Saloni, one of our marketing executives. We were all having a good time, and after a certain point, the others had gotten up to dance and the two of us were left at the table. I tried to get up but realized I had had one too many drinks and had to lean on her for support, to avoid falling. I sat back down on the bar stool and tried to get up again, a few minutes later, but was still unable to. It took me a few tries to actually get up, make it to the bathroom and then call a cab to take me home. She was there throughout, but at some point, she must have misconstrued something. I came to know that she had filed a complaint only a few days ago', he concluded.

'Do you have a copy of her complaint?' Atul nodded and handed the written complaint that he had all but memorized over to the lawyers. They sat in silence for about five minutes while the lawyers read the complaint, occasionally making notes and quietly talking amongst themselves. He kept looking at them, wondering what they were thinking and waiting for the inevitable questions to come. He had told himself to stay calm, but even after giving himself several pep talks, he felt unprepared for what was in store.

'It says here in the complaint, that you repeatedly squeezed the complainant's thigh while the two of you were sitting at the bar?' asked the lawyer. 'Well, I may have but I had no wrong intentions', replied Atul. 'As I said, I had drunk a little bit too much that night, like a lot of the other employees, and when I tried to get up, I found I couldn't balance myself—I reached out to balance myself and unfortunately, in my drunken state, I may have touched her leg by accident. There was no bad intent on my part', he repeated.

'Mr Menezes, we understand what you're saying but you need to be clear with us', replied the lawyer. 'There are some serious allegations of physical advances in this complaint and for us to defend you; you need to be prepared to answer all our questions as honestly as you can. There is no point in you repeating your story without providing adequate detail to counter what's in the complaint.' 'I will do my best', Atul said, bracing himself.

'What was the nature of your relationship with the complainant? What is her position in the organization, and does she report to you?' asked the lawyer. 'We apologize if you think these questions are invasive, but we need to have as much information as possible to contextualize the complaint and come up with a comprehensive defence. You could also tell us a little bit about yourself', she said.

Atul sighed. 'I had come to Bangalore as a young man in 1995, from Mangalore. I had always dreamed of starting my own company and decided that this was the place to do it. I gathered up my savings, found a small apartment in the city and set up my small business, which began to do quite well in a year or two. I hired my first full-time junior in 1997, and since then, our team has grown along with the business.'

'Saloni and I met in 2017, at a job fair. She had done her MBA from a reputed university and was looking for a job in Bangalore. Her family is from Mumbai, but she wanted to live away from them and live her own life. I saw a spark in her and told her to come in for an interview the next day', Atul said. 'We had a good conversation at the interview, and she joined us from the next month. She's also been doing quite well at the company', he said. 'In fact, she helped close the deal we were celebrating that night.'

'Have you ever had a romantic relationship with her or were either of you ever interested in each other?' asked the lawyer abruptly. 'Also, are either of you married or in relationships?'

'I have never been married', shot back Atul. 'And I know that she is not married either. We have never had an affair but have always been friendly acquaintances. That's why this complaint is such a shock', he said. 'We have never been very close, but I thought we shared a good working relationship with each other. I don't know if she has a boyfriend', he added.

'If the two of you weren't close, why were the two of you sitting alone at the bar? Is it a regular practice for you to visit bars with your subordinates?' asked the lawyer. Atul struggled to find the words to reply to this obviously leading question and finally said, 'Our office culture is different from other corporate workplaces. Even though we have a hierarchy on paper, most of us are very free and open with each other. I often hang out with employees after work, and they definitely hang out with each other. It's a very modern work culture where we discuss everything with each other in the office, and we end up drinking together too', he said.

'So if it's such a free culture, why do you think she filed the complaint?' asked the lawyer. This was the question that had baffled Atul, and no matter how much he thought about it, he was unable to come up with an answer that made sense. 'I don't know!' he finally burst out. 'I don't see what I did wrong that night. There were a lot of drunken people at that party who were way more hammered than I was, and I didn't see anyone else having a problem with the way they were behaving!'

The lawyer was quick to pick up. 'How was everyone else acting?' she asked. Atul tried to remember. 'Well, the table next to us was doing shots, and many of us were on the dance floor', he said. 'I don't remember exactly, but I know that a lot of them were drunk, including some of the boys who needed to be held and taken to their cabs. There were a few girls too, who were being supported by some of the boys because they were too tipsy to walk', he recounted. 'I don't feel like I was acting worse than any of them.'

'Do you feel like you were being targeted, then?' asked the lawyer. 'Is there any specific reason you can think of as to why anyone would want to target you?' she added. Atul thought about it. Out of his entire company, comprising of about 60 people, he had personally hired over 50 per cent as freshers or young professionals in their mid-20s, including Saloni. He had mentored many of these youngsters and felt proud of how, even though he was their boss, they treated him like a friend. Several of his employees had, over the years, confided in him about their personal problems, mental health issues and even their love lives, and he counted some of them as his close friends. He made it a point to know the office gossip, be part of the office jokes and act as an equal part of the team.

'No', he finally said. 'I have always been an understanding and approachable boss to these people', he said. 'I feel like many of them don't even see me as a boss but as a friend', Atul firmly stated. 'I can't think of any reason why Saloni would target me particularly, since we are actually friends. Or at least, I thought we were', he added lamely.

'I make it a point to talk to my employees, be supportive and not make them feel like I'm their boss or senior', Atul went on. 'I don't see myself as their boss but a part of the team. And I feel that even they see me that way, at least till now.'

'What is the average age of the office?' asked the lawyer. 'Do you think that you are treated differently because you're older?' This question threw Atul for a loop. He had to actually sit and think about it. 'I don't know', he finally said. 'I don't think so.' He tried to recount instances in the past where his age, which was almost twice the age of the employees, had been brought up but that was quickly replaced by a wave of resentment and anger. Why should he be the one sitting and overthinking when he was the one unfairly targeted? Why should he question himself when he had given this girl a great career and a whole life in a different city?

Atul caught himself being watched by the lawyers and said, 'I am about 48, and the average age of the office is between 23 and 32. It's common in start-ups', he added. When the lawyers didn't respond, he felt a mixture of fear and anger creeping upon him. 'Just because I'm a little older than them, suddenly, I'm the office pervert?' he asked, forcefully. 'I have given these kids such great opportunities! They're lucky to have a boss like me who's so liberal and understanding! You don't understand—this company exists because of me, because of all my hard work over so many years! And now, it'll all be thrown away because of one stupid incident? Because of one girl who couldn't understand our relationship, everything is ruined! Why did she have a problem with me when everyone else, when every other male at that party, was acting the same way? Why was Pradeep putting his arm around Aparna just friendly, but me resting my hand on Saloni for support suddenly 'sexual harassment'? It's just discrimination!' he blurted out. 'It makes no sense otherwise! They're just discriminating against their boss!'

Whenever Atul's narrative has been shared with an audience, the most common reaction has been, 'What made him do what he did? It was such a stupid thing to get drunk with an employee so much younger and then not being able to hold yourself....' One might wonder, for a man who is as successful as him, who enjoys warmth and respect from his colleagues in his organization and his industry, what could have made him do something that would eventually cost him his reputation, the respect that he has earned all through his life. In situations like this, many people would say 'men will be men, and no matter how much they have achieved and succeeded, they would take any opportunity to transgress boundaries almost like a privilege that they have earned'. This would trigger a counter-voice that would take on the #notallmen argument—that 'not all men transgress; in fact, statistically men who don't outnumber the men who do', etc.

Everyone has a back-story, and so does Atul. A young techie, who dreams of a life very different from the one he had seen in his family and community, comes to Bangalore. Life was never dull for a moment, he was attractive enough intellectually and physically, and in Bangalore, which had started attracting young people from across the country and the world, dating, relationships and sex were never a problem. And while he was never averse to marriage, it just didn't happen for various reasons, and he had no regrets about it. For him, his company and his organization was his psychological family and even though attrition and turnover were moderate, people would start their career in his organization and then move on to larger companies or venture on their own. He fostered a culture of informality, casualness and freedom and that never compromised on work or professional integrity. As he grew into his 40s, the age difference between him and the others in his organization kept getting wider, with the mean age of the others remaining at 27, and he started moving into 'the uncle zone'. He insisted on a first name culture and refused to be addressed as sir even by the interns. In other words, he was fighting to retain his youth, and not because he wanted to be young per se, he just didn't want to be distanced from others in the office. Office romance, dating and affairs were not uncommon in the organization, and in earlier years, there were women that Atul had dated and also had sexual relationships with and while a couple of them had gone sour because of reasons of incompatibility and the women had left, they had never been called sexual harassments, they were consensual relationships. However, as he grew older, Atul could feel that the women in his office, even if they called him by his first name, their warmth and affections were benign, asexual and that made him feel irritated, angry, sad and deeply envious of the other young men in the team in whom he could see his past days. None of this back-story recounting is intended to justify Atul's transgression but only to delve into his mind that would allow him to take a risk that seemed to be so difficult to rationalize.

Atul's disclosure to his lawyer leaked his indignation—why he was being singled out for something that seemed to be acceptable to the other men in the organization. Throughout his account, he seemed to be oblivious as to why the woman who filed the complaint against him would do so, especially because they shared a good working relationship. What Atul was not in touch with is his jealousy of other younger men, his demands of being given the same permissions and privileges that he sees them 'enjoying', he was clearly disconnected from the reality he is in, emotionally and psychologically.

Atul's claim of being framed is not attributed to the complainant's demand for money or any other motivation. He simply feels discriminated against and, therefore, singled out as 'an old pervert'. Atul is not patriarchal in the way his father or men in earlier generations were; he has not subscribed to normative demands of marriage, children—especially sons, creating heirs for the lineage or accumulation of wealth and property to assert social power. Yet he has grown up in transitional patriarchy wherein male sexuality thrives on feelings of power, assertion, entitlement to claim, desirability by younger (not older) women and virility of youth. Loss of youth that makes him less desirable to younger women, especially women who are on their journey of professional achievement and success in their own right, triggers fears of loneliness, isolation, redundancy and loss of one's mortality. His transgression onto a young woman stems from self-absorption and unattended and unresolved feelings, which were blind to the impact on the person at the receiving end. In another circumstance, a woman, who may have been afraid of the consequences of complaints, especially against the CEO and founding member, may have repressed the rage and shame.

Audits in organizations must adequately pay attention to men's issues, their vulnerability and transitions, which are often hidden because of denial. Mental health issues are a bigger stigma to men than to women because having mental health issues is socially seen to be a sign of weakness; it carries a real threat to one's career where the organizational culture may demand leadership where a leader cannot be seen to be going through emotionally or psychologically difficult stages. Therefore, a necessary step in talking about issues of gender and leadership is to talk about how the organization sees vulnerability and what biases it may carry when it sees vulnerability in men as opposed to vulnerability in women.

As much as we believe in keeping personal issues and matters separate from our professional lives, our psychological journeys in our life stages will necessarily impact who we are at our workplace. And it is not about being 'fixed' or normalized; our role-taking, leadership, interpersonal relationships and emotional and psychological needs will keep evolving, shifting and changing as we move through different life stages. In a corporate world, the demands to maintain a professional image makes it even harder to recognize and be in touch with how our internal world and our life space may be impacting our relationships and dealings with people in our workspace. Empathizing with men is not equal to softening the accountability of their transgressions or violations. Empathizing with men who suffer patriarchy in their own ways, that may make them more vulnerable to self-deception, is a necessary condition for achieving equitable gender dynamics in a workplace.

7

A MAN'S GAZE

Male gaze

male vulnerability

male victimhood

victim-perpetrator dichotomy

gender stereotypes

Why should sexual harassment policies only consider women as victims and men as perpetrators? This is a question every POSH trainer is asked in almost every training. And different trainers may have explanations that aim to rationalize and justify the policy stance or not. But here are two cases that provoke some thoughts and questions.

Mannan sat back in his airplane seat and reminisced about the past year. As an employee of a multinational consultancy based in Kolkata, his job had been quite stressful, especially over the past several months. His company was planning an international merger with another company in London, and Mannan and his team had been given the responsibility of overseeing the entire process. He thought about his very first briefing, where the division head had informed him and his team that if the merger was successful, it would be the largest international merger in a decade. From then on, the pressure was intense and the stakes were high.

Mannan had dived into his work for months, ignoring his friends, family and putting his social commitments on the back burner. And now, he thought to himself, everything was finally coming to fruition. After a final meeting in London, the papers would be signed at last, and he would be able to get back to his normal life, his friends and his on-again, off-again relationship.

After landing at London Heathrow, Mannan was picked up at the airport and taken straight to a four-hour meeting at the client's office. Exhausted and exhilarated after almost finalizing the deal, he was taken to spend the night at a two-BHK serviced apartment at the beautiful Canary Wharf. He was surprised to find it already occupied by a woman and even more taken aback to realize that she was no other than Ms Natalie Cruz. A successful venture capitalist, Natalie was a key stakeholder in the deal Mannan was working on, who had promised to invest over a quarter of a million pounds into the merger. She had attended the first half of the meeting but had left, citing other professional commitments. He had no idea that they were going to be staying at the same apartment for the duration of their stay, and it seemed, neither did she.

Mannan and Natalie greeted each other and made friendly small talk for a while. Mannan was surprised by how approachable and pleasant she was, behind the veil of professionalism and seriousness that had characterized all their previous meetings. In the evening, they sat down at their shared couch, poured some drinks and started talking, settling into surprising ease with each other. As the evening progressed, Mannan became painfully aware that Natalie had moved much closer to him on the sofa and seemed to be definitely interested. He felt a little conflicted and confused by her behaviour because they were also working on the merger together; but she seemed unbothered, smiling at him periodically and making dinner plans for the two of them.

After a few hours, Mannan was tired. He wanted to turn in as they had a long day tomorrow. When he stood up and told Natalie that he'd take her leave for the night, she forthrightly asked him if he'd be up to spending the night with her instead. Mannan hesitated. On one hand, he was not interested romantically or sexually in her at all. He was in a relationship back home and couldn't see beyond how unprofessional it would be to sleep with a colleague, even if it was just for a night. On the other hand, Mannan asked himself if refusing Natalie would really be the smartest thing to do. He thought of all the sleepless nights, working weekends and missed family commitments because of this merger. He looked at Natalie, who got up, took his hand and walked towards her open bedroom. 'Is it worth it to jeopardize the merger because I am being a prude?' he thought to himself. He was torn. However, after a few seconds, he sighed to himself and resignedly walked into the room behind her.

Two weeks later, Mannan sat at his new desk in his Mumbai office and asked his assistant for a cup of coffee. He was looking out of the window, admiring the view from his new office, when he heard someone come in and close the door. He turned around to find his friend, Sonia, looking very uneasy. 'So I've heard something', she started abruptly. 'I don't know if it's true but I thought I should talk to you.' 'What is it?' asked Mannan, slightly surprised. 'Is everything okay?' 'You tell me', said Sonia. 'I heard from someone at the London office that when you went to sign the merger, you met Ms Cruz?'

Mannan knew where this was going. 'Yes, you know I did, Sonia', he said. 'She was there at the meetings, as a key stakeholder. And yes, before you ask, we did stay at the same apartment.' 'Mannan, did anything happen between the two of you?' asked Sonia. 'I heard from Max at the London office, just an hour ago, that they'd seen the two of you together the next morning when they picked you up and it definitely looked like the two of you had something going on', she added.

Mannan smiled. 'What, really? I didn't think it was that obvious!' he said. Sonia looked disturbed. 'You cheated on Kanika, Mannan!' she said. She looked away. 'I know you weren't together all the time but didn't you think of her when you were in this situation?'

'Of course, I did, Sonia', replied Mannan. 'It wasn't like that. It's not like I initiated anything with that woman, she came on to me', he found himself saying. 'She was really blatant and basically led me into her bedroom. I wasn't even interested in sleeping with her!'

Mannan was surprised to see Sonia look aghast. 'What do you mean you weren't interested?' she said. 'Did she force you to do something?' she looked shocked. 'No, nothing like that!' he responded. 'Look, the deal was closing the next day, we were having a good time chatting and when she propositioned me, I didn't really know how to say no', he said. 'I didn't want to offend her and maybe screw up the merger, but she didn't force me to do anything. Let it go, Sonia', he said.

Sonia had no intention of letting anything go. 'Mannan, Max told me that you looked really tired and upset the next day', she said. 'Are you sure you were okay?' 'Of course, I am', he responded impatiently. 'It's not right for someone to gossip like this, you should tell Max to keep his mouth shut', he said. 'I was obviously tired the next morning because we hadn't slept much and yes, I was also feeling guilty and confused about what happened, but I'm over it', he said.

Sonia remained unconvinced. 'Mannan, if you didn't want to sleep with her but felt like you had no choice, that's sexual harassment', Sonia said seriously. 'She didn't have to force you physically to harass you.' 'Please, Sonia!' interrupted Mannan. 'You're being ridiculous, *yaar*! See, I didn't want to at first, fine. But then, I told myself that this woman is gorgeous, she's interested in me, commitment-free and other guys would kill for an opportunity to land someone like that. Also, she was in such a good mood, we closed the deal in record time the next day.' Sonia still looked sceptical. 'Come on Sonia', said Mannan. 'I may not have been on board at first but, at least, it was an experience.'

Alex and Pankaj were unlikely friends. Apart from the fact that they both worked in one of the leading boutique advertising agencies in Mumbai, they seemed to have nothing in common. Pankaj was in his mid-40s, loud, flamboyant and the creative director of the agency. He had been at the agency for over 20 years and was known for his loud, boisterous personality, his wild sense of humour and his crazy escapades at every agency party. Alex, on the other hand, was in his mid-20s and much quieter, with an easy smile and sarcastic sense of humour. He had just graduated from the National Institute of Design, and his final project had caught the eye of a senior person at the agency, who personally recommended that he be hired. He had joined the agency about eight months earlier and had, with his sweet personality, won over his colleagues. Without realizing, Alex had won over Pankaj, as well.

Alex's arrival at the agency caused a new kind of turmoil within Pankaj that he had never experienced before. Pankaj had been married (and divorced) twice, both times to wonderful women he was still friends with and had a spate of girlfriends while single. He had always considered himself firmly on the heterosexual side of the spectrum, but after Alex arrived, he couldn't explain the pull that drew them together. They struck up a firm but unlikely friendship, bonding over lunches, dinners, shared work trips to different cities; and after a few months, Pankaj realized that he had genuinely fallen in love with his young colleague.

Pankaj was initially worried that people would find out that he had fallen for Alex, but as they grew closer, he began to think that maybe Alex had feelings for him too. They became inseparable without ever saying a word to each other or confessing their feelings, and before long, their friendship was a subject of wide speculation in the agency. 'You think they're together?' became an oft-whispered topic between their colleagues but nobody ever had the courage to come out and ask Pankaj or Alex directly. Pankaj, at least, heard some of the whispers. He thought long and hard about how deeply he felt for Alex and realized that he wanted him in his life forever.

'What's the point living in the 21st century if I can't love whom I want to love, openly?' he asked himself and in true flamboyant fashion, began to plan how to woo the man he wanted to spend his life with. The next few months were a whirlwind for Pankaj. He started sending Alex little gifts at first—flowers, chocolates, short and sweet letters, brush pens, a scarf—little things that he knew Alex would appreciate. He started taking him out on dates to romantic, candlelit restaurants and even took a gourmet cooking class so he could cook them romantic meals at his place.

If those few months were a whirlwind for Pankaj, they were nothing short of a tsunami for Alex. Being used to a completely different vibe in university, he had initially struggled to find the perfect balance between 'professional' and 'fun' at his new workplace. When Pankaj had taken him under his wing, he had been relieved and grateful; relieved because he knew he was in the good books of the creative director, and grateful because Pankaj was genuinely a wonderful person, who Alex was able to rely on for warmth and care. He saw Pankaj as one of his best friends and a mentor of sorts, but after a few months, when he heard the rumours about them around work, he began to have second thoughts about their friendship. 'He's straight', he told himself firmly. 'None of these rumours is true, people just need something to talk about.' Although as time went on, the signs became more and more difficult to ignore. Alex saw the way Pankaj looked at him, the feeling behind the gifts he gave him and the efforts he made to make Alex happy; and as the weeks went past, Alex became more and more nervous about what Pankaj would do next. Even though he had experimented with men before, he wasn't ready for a relationship, that too, with a much older divorcee who happened to be his best friend. He put these thoughts out of his mind, though, trying to convince himself that Pankaj would never take things to the next step, trying to convince himself that Pankaj was straight, and all the rumours were untrue.

Things between Pankaj and Alex ended the way everyone expected them to—in disaster. One night, Pankaj cooked the two of them a romantic meal and proceeded to confess his love to Alex over their third glass of wine. Pankaj even had a ring in his pocket, which he showed Alex, saying that he could take it if he wanted—as a symbol of their love. Backed into a corner, Alex stammered out something about 'trying it out' and 'keeping it quiet', which really triggered Pankaj because after months of courting Alex and wooing him, his big moment had been marred by Alex suggesting that they have an illicit affair. Pankaj earnestly told Alex that he wanted to be with him, that he wanted to be his boyfriend/partner and be in a real relationship that they could eventually make official. He did not expect Alex to panic, pick up his bag and run out of the house—which he did.

The next day, the office was abuzz with gossip when Pankaj arrived. After a sleepless night spent alternatively trying to call Alex and dealing with his anguish, Pankaj was not ready for the news that Alex had handed in his resignation effective immediately. His friends at work told him sympathetically that Alex had come in early, requested a meeting with human resources where he had informed them that he would be leaving and had then disappeared without a trace. His phone was switched off, and he refused to answer emails or messages. Pankaj was distraught. To make matters worse, he was summoned by human resources the next day, to discuss his and Alex's relationship and what role it may have had in Alex's resignation.

The human resources personnel had talked at length about what Alex had said to them before quitting. He had said nothing to them about Pankaj but had appeared extremely distressed, saying that he had to get back to his family and, inadvertently, saying that it had been a 'mistake' for him to have joined the agency. They had a cursory meeting with Pankaj, who was dazed throughout and let the matter slide. However, nobody was prepared for the fallout of the entire incident. Once people found out that Alex had quit suddenly, they all started talking about how Pankaj must have professed his love to him, scaring him away. They had all been witness to Pankaj's developing feelings for the boy over several months, had seen many of the gifts delivered to Alex during working hours, and now, they were confident that he was behind the boy's hasty disappearance.

Pankaj, in all his misery, was shocked to realize that he was the prime topic of gossip at the office. He was even more shocked because he realized that Alex had never felt the same way about him. Pankaj, with a sinking heart, realized that Alex had always only looked at him as a friend. He had pursued this boy for months, not realizing that he was slowly backing him into a corner, leaving him no choice but to either agree to be with him or face the nasty repercussion of losing his mentor and best friend. Pankaj felt shame and guilt at how things had turned out, vowing to never repeat his mistake. He also marvelled at how people still laughed about it at parties, attributing Pankaj's actions to his 'craziness' and 'wild nature'. They even ventured to tease Pankaj about his 'failed attempt at being gay' and joked about keeping the male interns away from him. Pankaj played along and laughed at their jokes, going through the motions, with one thought being repeated over and over in his head—'Thank goodness Alex wasn't a woman!'

In every workshop where Mannan and Pankaj's stories have been shared, it met with an ambivalent response from the participants whether they necessarily qualify them as harassment, abuse, transgression or misconduct, or simply a matter of transaction between two individuals which is a private matter. Some people feel that what Mannan did was a matter of choice; he chose to have sex with Natalie for professional gain and pleasure. Many people feel irritated with Sonia's questioning him not short of badgering and trying to provoke something that is not there—guilt about infidelity, moral sanctions, trying to 'fit' the experience as sexual harassment where Mannan clearly denies so. It is also a pattern that more men feel this way and in every mixed group of participants, women are more curious about the reference to his disorientation the next day of the meeting.

There are a few common perceptions about male sexuality:

1. Men cannot be victims of sexual violence, particularly by women because no one can force them into erection unless they are turned on, and if they are sexually excited, then it is no longer abuse.
2. Men look for sexual opportunities so any offer of a sexual encounter, particularly from a woman he may find attractive, would be evoking his libido.
3. If a woman has propositioned a man, it cannot be sexual abuse because even if he rejects, she would not be able to use it against him. The stigma of abuse always sticks with women, not with men. Women get scored, and men score. So the active agent cannot be abused.
4. Mannan's excuse of not rejecting Natalie in the apprehension of the impact on the deal was only an excuse to justify the sexual escapade that he wanted. It may have been a way for him to rationalize his infidelity.

These notions are not only held by women about men, but men also believe the same. It becomes starker when one hears of a case like a 15-year old boy who was seduced by his 35-year old aunt, while he was staying with them for a holiday. This boy, after 20 years, visits a therapist when he was having marital problems and trust issues with his wife. Months of therapy unravelled how that sexual experience—which he would wear on his sleeve to brag to his friends about his 'Mrs Robinson story'—left traumatic imprints on him; his guilt about having cheated his uncle, him feeling sexually objectified when the aunt behaved as if nothing had happened the next morning and, thereafter, his subsequent sexual fixations with women much older to him and, subsequently, him finding it difficult to trust his wife and feeling emotionally frozen with her. It was very hard for him to acknowledge that he had no power or consent in the sexual encounter, he was taken by surprise and shock, he was sexually aroused with her when she made her move, but he never understood why she did what she did, whether there was any attraction she had felt towards him or whether he was just a tool for her masturbation. As a reader, it becomes easier to recognize abuse, because first, in this case, the person was underage at the time, and second, there was no consent of any kind. But the issue is that he found it difficult to recognize it as abuse because he was sexually aroused, he was erect, he penetrated her and in doing so, he lost any claim to victimhood in his mind. Ultimately, only Mannan would know how that experience with Natalie had left him and cognition often takes longer to catch up with trauma. But what we do know with victims of sexual harassment or abuse is that cognition lags behind trauma. The victims of sexual exploitation in the Jeffrey Epstein case, for example, took months or years to realize telltale signs of emotional trauma—self-loathing, anger with oneself, uncontrollable mood swings, flashbacks and psychosomatic symptoms—which seemingly had nothing to do with their sexual encounters with Epstein or his other associates. In those situations, the encounters seemed transactional, with consent, exchange of money and no overt use of physical violence or torture. It would take Mannan to revisit and recount his emotional experience of that night to unravel what he may have experienced and where his own volition and power had been in that encounter.

Reporting of sexual harassment by men when the perpetrator is another man and where the victim identifies himself as heterosexual or has not disclosed his sexual orientation to the organization is a double whammy. This is an urban woke group of people who are progressive and are open enough to acknowledge fluidity of sexual orientation. However, what is instructive about the whole case was the aftermath of Alex's resignation where Pankaj's colleague summarized the entire incident as Pankaj's crazy infatuation and the object of his infatuation being too overwhelmed to deal with it and leaving. Pankaj's mutter to himself, where he thanks his lucky stars about Alex not being a woman, implied that he knew that the entire episode may have well qualified as sexual misconduct, if not harassment, had Alex been a woman. Alex's backend story was simple. He was not sure how to deal with it, and he was not convinced whether it even would qualify as transgression. He felt that he had played his part by participating in all close encounters with Pankaj, the socializing, the dinners, the after-office drinks, the movies on weekends, that he had long before transgressed a strictly professional relationship with him to now claim foul. A part of him felt very guilty and responsible, where he blamed himself for not having seen it coming, for leading on Pankaj and not being able to express his discomfort and anxiety when Pankaj had started courting him to romantic dinners and sending him gifts. It is socially and politically a very live discourse that women in Alex's position, despite doing all of that, could well have refused Pankaj's proposal and slapped a case of sexual harassment if Pankaj would have turned vindictive or the rejection would have had any adverse impact from Pankaj. However, sexual violence discourses, where men are victims, are poorly developed. There are very few researches on the subject of sexual vioelnce on men. Sexual harassment laws are presently exclusive to women, and any issues of sexual harassment between men will get labelled as LGBTQIA issue, which it may not be.

One of the areas that companies need to work with, therefore, is looking at the intersection between their diversity policy and sexual harassment policy and ensure that there is clarity on conditions where people may be of the same gender. Also, there need to be distinctions made between sexual misconduct and sexual harassment for people to not get caught with whether their discomfort qualifies as harassment or not.

Last, while the POSH advises companies to have workshops as a preventive strategy, once a year workshops or induction workshops followed by the policy are, as we can see across countries, highly ineffective in any systemic transformation of an organization. Rather than deriving activity checklists as a resource, organizations should look at a holistic design including, and not restricted to, a multi-media communication programme and a mix of online and onsite interventions.

8

BEING ILLEGAL

Homosexuality

criminalization

homophobia

transgender community

transphobia

microaggressions

non-conformity

In 1997, the Supreme Court of India made a ruling in response to a public interest petition asking for rights for women to work with safety and protection from harassment, termed as the Vishakha Guidelines. In 2013, the government passed the law on sexual harassment. Meanwhile, the Delhi High Court decriminalized consensual same-sex relationships in 2009, which was overturned by the Supreme Court in 2013, and finally, the Supreme Court itself decriminalized same-sex relationships in 2018. This is a case of 2016, when Section 377 of the Indian Penal Code was in force, criminalizing same-sex consensual relationships.

Leaving Ranchi and moving to Chennai was a big and exciting step for Naresh. At 22, he felt he wanted to start his life in a big city, far away from home and the community that he has grown up in. He wanted anonymity, where he could start afresh, with new people who would not know his parents or the family he belonged to, would not judge him by conservative morals and where he could find freedom—to grow, explore and discover. He thought he was lucky to get an offer from a start-up company that wanted to get into the business of organizing funerals and using technology to make it easier for people in small families to manage logistics. At first, the idea sounded morbid. Death and funerals were the last things on his mind, even though there have been times in his growing up years when he thought he felt suicidal. But he was never sure whether he was serious in his contemplation of death, or was it a drama that he wanted to see in his imagination of how his family, friends and bullies, nosy neighbours, loveable and nasty teachers and loving or horrible relatives, everyone would rue after him, repenting their acts of indifference, unfairness and meanness, mourning their loss. He suspected that, perhaps, he loved himself too much to take the risk of an uneventful death. Anyway, the good thing was that the company had a few other recruits from Jharkhand, and so he knew that he would not find himself completely alone as a Hindi speaking newbie amongst *Madrassis* as his mum refers to the Tamils.

It took him a few weeks to settle in. His boss and the company's proprietor helped him find a paying guest (PG) accommodation close to the office. Of the other boys who came from Jharkhand, one of them, Jayant, shared the room with him. Kunal and Shekhar found accommodation in a nearby house, less than a kilometre away. The owners of both houses were from Tamil families, both elderly couples whose children lived in various countries across the world—the USA, Europe and Australia. The boys secretly joked amongst themselves that their landlords might soon become clients of their company, since the children would have to depend on someone to arrange for the funerals when one or both of their parents passed away.

Life was treating Naresh well. He liked hanging around with the boys, for the most part. They always liked to stick to this group, but Naresh wanted to make new friends, get to know people in Chennai. His purpose of coming to Chennai, far away from home was not to be restricted to a small group of his own home folks but to get to know people from a different culture and, therefore, discover something for himself. Also, Naresh was gay, something he could never share with anyone in Ranchi. He dared not tell any of his friends or cousins, nor his parents. He feared the consequences which he did not know what they could be. Nothing is more terrifying, perhaps, than unknown consequences of an action. So part of his reason coming to Chennai was to get onto gay networking apps and meet people, date them and explore his own sexual orientation.

As months passed on, two things happened. First, he got into a rhythm at work. As a young tech-team, they learnt to work as a team, discovering each of their potentials and strengths and, therefore, leverage on them. Naresh was great in research—he had skills in finding out tech solutions, innovations and new discoveries in any part of the world, and spot what could be relevant to their business and bring ideas of adaptation to the table. As colleagues, they started developing respect for each other, and as friends, they started trusting each other. The second thing that happened was, Naresh disclosed his sexuality to Jayant, Kunal and Shekhar. It happened on an evening when the four of them had gone to a bar and had gotten drunk. Over alcohol, they started sharing about their personal lives, problems at home, with families, about their past, their dreams for themselves, about girls and their crushes. Jayant had a girlfriend from school, who had now completed her graduation and her family was trying to get her married off. Jayant knows that his girlfriend will not be able to stall the marriage for long and he, at the threshold of his career, would not be financially stable for at least another four–five years. This leads to frequent arguments and fights between them where Jayant wants Shikha, his girlfriend, to come over to Chennai with a job but she fears that her family will never allow this. She insists that he must convince his parents to speak to hers and convince them. She believes that even if they can offer engagement between them, her parents may agree to their match. Kunal spoke about his feelings of inadequacy with his looks. He was not good looking by conventional standards, and whenever he felt attracted to any girl in his neighbourhood or college or his social circle, they rejected him, and each rejection led him to feel smaller and smaller. At a moment, he broke down and said, 'The only hope for someone as *ugly* as me is to become rich so that I can be eligible if not for my looks but the financial affluence that I can offer to a girl.' Shekhar was not in any critical life space, but he seemed genuinely affected by the sadness and frustrations that his friends shared. He spoke about how he feels so much at home with the three of them, that they have become the source of his emotional stability where their joy and sadness, frustrations and hope affect him, and he would do anything in his power to be by their side, knowing that he, when in times of trouble, could find support from them too. It was in such a vulnerable moment that Naresh said that he had a confession to make. The others looked at him in silence, and when Naresh spoke about his attraction for men, they fell silent. After a few uncomfortable moments of silence, Jayant broke the silence with a completely unrelated issue from work. The obvious diversion of the subject, with no seeming outright rejection or affirmation of Naresh's disclosure, left him feeling anxious. He knew that he probably made a mistake by sharing something that his friends could not digest. For the other three boys, it was as if they had not heard Naresh at all.

Naresh was right. The impact of his disclosure was gradual but obvious. For starters, Jayant started avoiding any conversation with him when they were in their room. As soon as the two of them were in the room by themselves, he would immerse himself in watching a movie on his computer with headphones or be absorbed in surfing or chatting on his phone. If Naresh tried to initiate any conversation, he would respond in monosyllables. After a week of this frozenness between the two of them, Naresh asked him timidly one day if everything was all right between the two, and Jayant said, 'Of course!' with utter nonchalance. What was clear to Naresh was that nothing was the same between them as before. And that Jayant did not wish to talk about it or engage with him at any level. The next thing that happened was that in the weekends, Jayant, Shekhar and Kunal started excluding him from their plans. They would make plans to go out, watch movies or simply hang out in malls or in the beach but not tell Naresh. If Naresh started asking them about their plans for the weekend, they would make excuses and avoid him. Frequently, Jayant started sleeping over at Kunal and Shekhar's. One day, Jayant was shaving in the bathroom before his bath. Naresh had already had a bath, and he wanted to take his wet towel that he had left in the bathroom. The bathroom door was unlocked, and it was quite customary for either of them to also enter the bathroom for whatever reason. That day too, Naresh pushed the door open to reach out for his towel and Jayant yelled at him asking him to leave him alone. Naresh was stunned and it took him a while to realize that Jayant had set new boundaries for himself, he had stopped changing or even changing his clothes in front of Naresh. While earlier, he would sleep bare bodied and complained about the Chennai heat, he now would always wear a t-shirt and track pants even at night. It dawned on him suddenly that Jayant may be insinuating that Naresh was a sexual predator and trying to seduce him. He felt so humiliated and small; that night, he felt like killing himself. Only this time, the fantasy was not followed by any sequence of people mourning his death. He just wished that a cold and dark night would envelop him, and he could disappear in it, like in a black hole.

At work, things started becoming awkward. Naresh started feeling isolated. Even when he offered them information that he gathered from his research, they appeared cold and uninterested. They started making him feel redundant. He would sit in his desk and have lunch, no one called him and if he tried joining a huddle, everyone would disperse. Gradually, things got worse for him. There would be a lot of homophobic jokes and jibes flung around, not directly at him. He would often hear 'here comes the homo' when he walked by or approached anyone. Avoidance and passive aggression soon turned into active bullying, stigmatizing and name-calling.

Within a matter of days, what seemed to have been fostering as a close emotional bond between Naresh and his three friends had turned into a hostile relationship, extremely passive-aggressive and humiliating for him. He was steeped in guilt and shame and angry with himself that he should have never disclosed his personal matter to his friends. He could not concentrate at work; he lost his appetite, and his emotional distress started showing in his work. Naresh's boss, Ram Subramaniam, who was in his early-30s, with whom they had a relationship like a college senior and had elements of reverence and peerage at the same time, noticed the change in his behaviour and his work. Ram called him over to his room one day and gave him feedback about his work. He said that he had been noticing that Naresh was distracted and the quality of his work had fallen drastically. While he was concerned for Naresh, he also made it clear that as a start-up, he could not afford sloppiness and non-performance and unless Naresh did something about it soon, he may have to let him go. Naresh kept quiet; his gaze steadfast on his feet. After a few moments of silence, Ram asked impatiently what the problem was and that if there was anything about the office or his colleagues, he should share it, else Ram could not help him even if he could. Naresh thought he had nothing to lose. 'If I tell Ram, it can go any which way. Either he will be sympathetic and understand my problem and help find a solution, or he, like the others, will stigmatize me. If I do not say anything, nothing will change, and I will lose the job anyway.

When Ram heard what had happened, he kept quiet for a while. And his first words were, 'What you are talking about, Naresh, is illegal. You could be arrested and put behind bars for this. Do you realize that what you have shared is not only illegal; if the word should get out, it will bring great shame upon your family and disrepute to our company? What were you thinking when you 'disclosed' your sexual orientation to your friends? What did you expect from them? You should have gone to a psychiatrist, or a doctor or counsellor to fix your problem. Instead, while they were speaking about their girlfriends and marriage, you decided to bring your homosexuality into the discussion, thereby equating their heterosexuality with your homosexuality. Do you expect it to be the same?'

At the time of this incident, homosexuality had not been decriminalized by the Supreme Court of India. The 2009 Delhi High Court judgement that decriminalized sex between consenting adults between same sexes in private, had been challenged in the Supreme Court which had held it to be well within the purview of Section 377 of the Indian Penal Code in 2013, which criminalized homosexual relations in private. However, proponents for decriminalization of homosexuality had filed a curative petition in 2016, which finally got a verdict in favour of the decriminalization in June 2018. Naresh's incident in Chennai was in 2017 while the matter was still hanging in the Supreme Court of India.

Ram's response left Naresh stunned. Not only was he prejudiced against homosexuality, but also he was literally calling him a criminal and had no empathy for Naresh's struggle with bullying and stigma that he was facing at work. He apologized to Ram, for what, he was not sure, but that moment, the 'Sorry!' carried words, thoughts and emotions that he could not possibly articulate. He was sorry that he had trusted Ram and had hoped any help from him. He was sorry for having disclosed his sexuality to his colleagues and friends. He was sorry that he was not 'strong' enough to not care about the stigma and bullying and continue to work and produce results. He was sorry that he had put himself in this situation and given the power to others to make him the way he was feeling. And most of all, he was sorry that for the first time in his life, he started feeling that he was cursed.

Naresh resigned from his job the next day. He sent his resignation by email and did not wait for a response. He packed his bags and left the PG accommodation the very next day telling the landlord that there was a crisis at home and he had to return urgently. He thought of leaving a note for Jayant. He sat with his pad and pen for an hour, and he could not move his pen. All he could put down were his tears on that paper, and he left that soaked and dried crumpled piece of paper on the table.

Naresh finally returned to Ranchi. He had joined a non-profit that works on education. He had taken a foolish chance of disclosing his sexuality in this organization from the start. And the organizational chief hugged him hard and assured him of all support, in case he ever felt marginalized or stigmatized in this organization. At the end of the day, Naresh learnt the hard way that urbanity, exposure to modern education or being a millennial had no bearing on how liberal they might be towards taboos. One finds liberalism where one expects it least.

Naresh did not know if there was any sexual harassment committee in that start-up. They were never informed of it, even if there was. Does his experience even qualify as a matter of sexual harassment? The law on sexual harassment in India is restricted to sexual harassment of women; it does not include sexual harassment of men. How should organizations and companies deal with cases of homophobia within their organizations?

Diversity and inclusion policies in several multinationals have a policy of non-discrimination on grounds of caste, class, religion, ethnicity and sexual orientation. The Indian constitution also strongly condemns discrimination, stigma and untouchability, which was, at the time, stated explicitly to prevent abuse and exploitation of Dalits. Modern organizations, however, will have to confront issues of discrimination, prejudice and stigma on the basis of sexual orientation, especially now that the Supreme Court has read down Section 377 of the Indian Penal Code that criminalized same-sex relations between consenting adults (2018 judgement, in response to the curative petition). It is incumbent upon organizations and companies to protect their employees from sexual harassment on grounds of sexual orientation as well.

Since 2018, several large corporates have taken strident steps to include sexual minorities in their companies not only by extending insurance covers and health benefits to partners, but also taken strategies from leadership buy-in on inclusion to creating support groups for LGBT people and people who are not queer, creating buddy systems between people of different sexual orientations. And to put an end to harassment and abuse, several companies have also adopted 'zero tolerance' policies.

Sharmila is a transwoman, 27 years of age. She considers herself lucky and fortunate to have been able to move through school, college and university and bag herself a job in a company with one of the most progressive LGBTQIA+ (lesbian, gay, bisexual, transgender, queer, intersex, asexual) policies in the country. She was happy to attend support group meetings and had been assigned a buddy who was senior to her, Sushil Mishra, who assured her all help and support if she ever found herself in any difficult situation. All through school, college and university, she had presented as a male, despite knowing that she was a woman, and it was only when she applied for her job that she felt safe enough to openly identify as a transgender since the company had a stated non-discrimination policy for sexual minorities. When she finally got the job, it was a big step for her to finally dress the way she wanted and come to work, something which she could only do for social events in LGBT support communities.

In the initial days, she used to be very self-conscious about how others looked at her, how they stared at her. At 5 feet 10 inches, she stands tall, even compared to men in India and as a woman, she draws attention from a distance. She has not surgically transitioned yet, something she has planned a couple of years later, once she had saved the money for it, even though the insurance will pay 50 per cent of the reassignment surgery cost up to 2 lakhs. She has had a cordial, formal interface with her team leader, Arun Pandey, who never looked at her directly while he spoke. But then, she realized, Arun had poor eye contact with most people, and she may not be the exception. Her other team members were friendly, particularly the women. The men in the team were friendly and polite, albeit a little cautious, which she could understand. In some ways, they (the male colleagues) could not sometimes figure out whether they should be casual with her 'as a man' (sharing the so-called 'male-humour') or treat her 'like a lady'. While they could casually flirt with the other single women, their conversations with her would never ever have any streak of flirtation. Sharmila is pragmatic; she understands that if she gets caught up with these issues, she would never be able to assimilate in any professional team. However, it did occur to her that perhaps in the mind map, she was of a 'third gender', even though she did not see herself that way.

Over time, she focused on her work. Diligence and discipline have pulled her through many hard situations in life of discrimination, abuse, harassment by peers, authority figures and even her parents. This job was her break, and she told herself that if she could play this right, she would never have to look back again. Teamwork is what helped her build relationships with her peers. Arun, Ravi, Sanjay, Mayank, Priyanka, Manasi and Snigdha all realized how dependable she was and was always willing to cooperate with and help others if she could. They found her sweet and the women felt sympathetic to her, and they had started hanging out together. Although she had always identified herself as a girl, a woman, Sharmila also realized some differences between how she looked at femininity and how the others looked at femininity. For example, many of the other girls, all in their 20s, seemed to be very cautious about boundaries with their male colleagues and even if they were attracted to them, they would always take extra measures to appear inaccessible to them. It was not something Sharmila could identify with; if she felt attracted to any of her male colleagues, she found herself far from expressing it, because she knew that it would never be reciprocated, at least, not as a legitimate relationship. But her context was different from their context.

However, she realized that like her, the others have also had abusive experiences being sexually touched and abused in public transport and sometimes even by neighbours, relatives or older cousins. For Sharmila, the abuse was always much more severe, she felt while listening to them. She suspected that if the others had any plans of grouping in any one of their homes, they did so in private and not in front of her; perhaps, they would be embarrassed if she would go to their families.

The events and the interventions of the LGBTQIA+ support group were mostly attended by some of the community members. Even though events would be open to all, others would also be explicitly invited, and managers would be told to send their supervisees, if they came at all—it was more out of obligation than interest. Even though the organizing team did their best and it did include some members who are gay, bisexual or transgender themselves and some others from the HR department who were straight (mostly women), they turned out to be superficial, politically correct and often sermonizing.

On one occasion, Sharmila had been assigned a task in which she was to co-work with Ravi. She liked Ravi, he was fun, always cracking the stupidest of jokes and although he took some time to find ease with her, over the months, he had grown to be pretty comfortable with her and she with him. The task went off very well and upon submission, they received very positive feedback from Mr Pandey with one of his rare smiles. Ravi shook hands with her and said, 'You and I make a good team, Shy!' She unexpectedly found herself tearing up and quickly excused herself to the washroom. When she was on her way back to her seat, she suddenly heard Mayank and Sanjay teasing Ravi about his partnership with Sharmila and just as she entered the cubicle, Ravi, who had his back towards her, screamed at them saying, 'Dude, I connect with her with my intellect, not with my dick for her ass!' The moment of discomfort that ensued could have curdled fresh milk. Sharmila felt like she had been punched in the gut. She could do nothing at that moment except look at the floor, at the cubicle walls, at anything except these men and seeing her come in, the conversation disbanded almost immediately, with everyone acting like nothing had happened.

Later that night, as Sharmila was lying listlessly in her bed, she thought to herself that she mustn't ever let her guard down if she had to protect herself from being insulted. She tried to tell herself that this was a situation where everyone had a location of their own that was not marked with hatred. Mayank and Sanjay could have jibed Ravi if the same situation had happened with Priyanka instead of Sharmila and Ravi would have joked back. Ravi is not transphobic, Sharmila tried to tell herself. This was the first time in his life he was engaging and finding ways of connecting with a person from whose community, he has only seen as a '*hijra*' as objects of stigma and social outcasts. But if his warmth towards Sharmila should 'taint' his sexuality, that scared him because he knew what the stigma of a 'gay man' carries. And in this case, Sharmila was not a man, so what would that make him? Every time Sharmila embarked on this train of thought, she was uncomfortably forced to acknowledge that yes, even if Ravi did not openly acknowledge it, he was definitely still transphobic, and insidiously so.

The LGBT assimilation programme in organizations needs to go further than a moral endorsement from leaders, equal opportunity and benefits and recruitment and basic safety measures. Assimilation approaches and strategies to combat stigma have worked well in several other anti-stigma programmes by mental health and social action groups, and here are five approaches which could be tried:

1. Qualitative research: Questions on how assimilation and engagement experiences have been for people of different sexualities and gender identities, what have been some of the discoveries of the new of self and the other, or what have been the challenges or struggles experienced; can be safer ways of gauging which stage of assimilation the LGBTQI groups have reached.
2. Sharing research findings: Research findings can trigger interesting questions and if a communication strategy was to be evolved from it, it would transform the discussion spaces from being moral, righteous and dry to being more vibrant and relevant to everyone as well as engaging.
3. Experiential workshops or labs: Experiential workshops on gender and sexuality and identity are useful as a personal growth programme, not necessarily only pertaining to LGBTQI inclusion and assimilation but also to work with disowned or repressed parts of oneself.

4. Case conferencing: One does not always have to have experiences like Sharmila's to be reported. Research findings should lead to case studies which, with care to protect the confidentiality, may be used for case conferencing and analysis and experimentations.
5. Talk about heterosexuality and heteronormativity: Assimilation of LGBTQIA+ people in the workplace has as much to do with heterosexuality and heteronormativity as it does with understanding queerness. The focus does not need to be only on the 'minority group', but with the dominant culture as well. Explore how does a heteronormative space respond when it invites a non-heteronormative group as a part of its inclusion principles.

9

PERSONAL VERSUS PROFESSIONAL: CONFLICT IN NON-PROFITS

Non-profits

false righteousness

organizational safety

suppressed transgressions

external activism

Anisha Ratnam, the founder of Womxn First, a prominent women's rights non-governmental organization (NGO), walked into their Mumbai office one Monday morning to find a senior colleague, Zainab Adil, anxiously waiting for her in her office. 'Morning, Zainab, is everything okay?' Anisha asked, putting her bag down and standing at her desk. 'Anisha, I wanted to speak to you about something urgent and it couldn't wait', said Zainab. 'I was operating the survivor help-line last night when a woman called to report that she'd been sexually harassed at work. The ICC in her company dismissed her complaint, and now she wants to take further action.'

'So let's help her', said Anisha, surprised. 'Zainab, this is not an unusual type of call', she continued. 'You know that the survivor helpline is for all victims of sexual harassment and violence and that we help them with counselling, legal and social services.' 'Yes, Anisha, I know that', said Zainab. 'The issue here is that the person who sexually harassed her is a senior-level male employee from Samvoday Technologies Private Limited.' She fell silent.

Anisha stopped short. She fell very silent for a few seconds and then just said, 'Oh', and fell silent again. She sat in her chair and motioned for Zainab to take a seat. 'Do they know the name of the sexual harasser?' she asked Zainab. 'Yes, it's a senior manager called Manoj something', said Zainab. Anisha involuntarily took a breath. Samvoday Technologies was her husband Ryan Bangara's company. He had founded the company about 25 years earlier and had built it into a successful business, facing a lot of struggles along the way. Even now, he was the acting CEO and chairman, and his company was his life.

This made things complicated. She needed time to think. 'What's the survivor's name?' she asked. 'What did she say about the harassment?'

'The survivor, Aarti Katyal, said that the harassment lasted for several months. Unsolicited attention, indirect demands to spend time with him, and he apparently offered to take her out a few times', recounted Zainab. 'And since he's such a senior employee, Aarti is saying that the ICC just ignored a lot of facts to find him innocent. She said that apparently, he's been on paid leave for almost two weeks now. She's really traumatized, Anisha', said Zainab.

'What does she want to do next?' asked Anisha. 'She wants to challenge the decision of the ICC in the High Court, and she wants help going to the media', said Zainab. 'She's a single mother with a small child, so she may also need some job counselling', she mused.

Anisha didn't say anything. She seemed to be deep in thought. After a few minutes of silence, Zainab suddenly spoke up. 'I know that this is a personal conflict, so I brought it to you as a friend, Anisha', she said abruptly. Anisha just stared at her. 'Just think about it and see how you want to handle this. You and Ryan are friends of mine, so I've brought this to you first', said Zainab. 'I won't ask the survivor to meet us just yet, but you have to handle it soon.' She left the room.

Anisha took a few moments to compose herself after Zainab left the room. She felt deeply conflicted and was surprised at herself for actually being in a dilemma. She had founded this organization in 2001 to work with oppressed women and had built it from the ground up into one of Mumbai's most active NGOs. Now, they had volunteers doing social work, counselling and therapy, pro bono legal work, handicraft classes, media and activism campaigns and helping with childcare all over the city. Anisha herself was at the forefront, the face of the organization and was quite a prominent figure in Mumbai and on social media.

What Anisha was most proud of was that women from all backgrounds and gender-variant persons who self-identified as women came to Womxn First for help. The organization was famous for being a safe space and accessible to any woman in need. This was Womxn First's philosophy.

'Yes, that was my philosophy, so that's how it became the organization's philosophy too', thought Anisha to herself. 'But what do I do now? If we take her case forward, then that'll mean one big media frenzy, lots of attention on Samvoday Tech....' She was fully aware that this would also mean that all eyes would be on her as well. As the face of the organization, she'd be expected to speak to the media, stand by the victim at all times and take the harasser and the company to court—all while her husband would be on the other side. She thought about the strain it would put on their marriage and felt physically sick. 'What do I do?' she thought.

'On the other hand, if we don't take her case forward, we avoid all that media nonsense', thought Anisha to herself. 'But then if we don't take her case then we'd have to turn her away', she thought. 'And what reason do we give her? We can't just say no without giving her a reason, and we've never turned anyone away before.' Anisha sighed and covered her face with her hands. 'We'll have to figure something out.'

'What do you mean you recuse yourself?' exclaimed Zainab. The others in the room also had disapproving expressions. Anisha got a little ruffled. 'You know exactly what I mean, Zainab', she said. 'Let Aarti's case be taken forward but by some other organization or activists. We can't just send her away, so I think we should help her out by organizing a proper alternative. We can liaise with people we know from other organizations and make sure that she gets the help she needs. We tell her why we choose to not get involved and leave it at that.'

'Tell me, why do 'we' choose to not get involved? Sounds more like you don't want to get involved', broke in Pinky. A prominent activist, Pinky worked with Womxn First on certain cases where the women were particularly vulnerable. She and Anisha had known each other for two decades and were good friends, for the most part. 'Actually, that's not the right question. How can we choose to not get involved? Women like her are why this organization functions, Anisha.'

'Pinky, you know exactly why we can't get involved', said Anisha. 'We have to make this choice based on the welfare of the organization as well. We don't need any media scandal surrounding us! We are doing good work here. We do what we do, and we speak up when necessary, in the interest of the women who come to us. Getting caught up in some media frenzy based on something that is a non-issue will just take away everything good that we are doing', she said.

'I'm sorry, Anisha, but I disagree', chimed in Rupa, one of their legal consultants. 'Firstly, this is not a non-issue. If it were, we wouldn't even be in this meeting!' Several others nodded. 'See, this is a conflict of interest for you, we can all see that. But I personally feel that you choosing to recuse yourself, and by extension, the whole organization, is just a little convenient. Don't you think so?'

'How is it convenient?' replied Anisha, aghast. 'It's a personal conflict of interest, because it's my husband's company', she said. 'Of course, when personal clashes with professional, the most logical thing to do is to remove ourselves from the situation. That's all we are doing here!'

'Come on, Anisha', said Pinky. 'You started this organization on a set of personal principles and clear political views which the organization shares. For you, personal has always been mixed with professional. You're suddenly setting boundaries now, which just seem a little convenient.' 'Yes, it's one thing to recuse yourself from being part of the POSH Committee in Samvoday Tech, but to deny a survivor of harassment your resources and help is just on another level, Anisha', said Rupa.

'I understand where you all are coming from', said Anisha. 'As an activist organization, we definitely blur the personal and the political, but we need to put some processes in place so that the work we do isn't at our own expense.' She looked around helplessly. 'This is definitely an ethical dilemma for me, which is why I chose to take myself out of the equation.'

'This actually begs an important, larger question', interjected Zainab. 'We need to engage with ethical conflicts that we have, not just distance ourselves from them. If we keep talking about Womxn First being a completely inclusive, accessible space, then we have to take a stance when a conflict arises. We can't afford to run away from this.'

Anisha sighed. 'Just because we stand for human rights, I guess that doesn't automatically mean that we are free from ethical dilemmas stemming from conflict between the ideological and one's personal life.'

NGOs or non-profits often generate this 'image' or evoke an expectation from outsiders of ethicality and righteousness behind all of their actions and activities. However, the reality on the inside of such organizations, as illustrated by Anisha's story, can show that several dilemmas and conflicts, blurring of notions of 'personal' and 'professional' can occur in abundance, even here.

A prominent NGO, working on gender justice and violence against women for several decades in India, was the subject of widespread gossip and rumours due to the late founder's ex-husband, whom we can call Amit. Amit's late wife, Dipika, had founded the organization, Survivor Rights (SR) in 2000 and both their lives revolved around it. Amit was integrally involved in managing SR too, but his wife was the face of it. Over the years, as their son and other family members joined SR and Dipika became internationally renowned as an 'expert' in women's rights, it took a toll on their marriage. Amit started to have an affair with Sakshi, Dipika's second-in-command at SR when Dipika went abroad on a three-year contract for a project. Amit and Sakshi continued their affair for over 12 years, until Dipika passed away in 2014. After her death, Amit and Sakshi continued to see each other until he suddenly announced his marriage in 2017 to someone else.

Sakshi spoke out to a number of activists and friends in the organization after Amit's marriage. Her feelings of betrayal and disappointment were communicated vocally, with her feeling as Amit's mistress, after so many years of being together—when he was married to Dipika and even after her death. While Amit's actions and Sakshi's hurt generated lots of gossip and rumours within the organization and activists' social spaces, it has notably not generated any conversation on boundaries, appropriateness and office cultures. Although many such organizations perpetuate ideologies to outsiders, it can be seen that not defining boundaries and not formulating and adhering to a set of organizational values can result in murky situations.

Organizations and individuals who work with gender violence and women's rights are not immune to transgression and violations. It may seem that many of these organizations are blind to gender politics within their organizations or averse to engage with them for fear of embarrassment, shame and losing credibility. That is because NGOs are often projected as beacons of righteousness by others, something which NGOs interject and internalize. That leaves the organization very little space and humility to acknowledge that like any other organization, it will too struggle with gender politics and often be caught unaware about transgressions under its very nose.

Anisha was vulnerable to being torn apart by her activist colleagues in the sector. And that is what happened eventually when they accused her of failing to live by the principles she would preach to others while advocating for people to take a righteous stand for women who are victims of abuse, even if it meant that perpetrators were your husband, sons or brothers. Womxn's experience is not rare or uncommon in the sector. Most activists who have worked against class-, caste- or gender-based violence are likely to have confronted situations in their personal lives that have threatened them to compromise with their ideologies for the sake of their immediate family—children, spouses or siblings in particular. A way out of these entrapments is to recognize and acknowledge how even activist organizations are not devoid of their own vulnerabilities and transgressions, how they are also likely to grapple with the same issues as any other organization and leaders in the corporate sector. This must be recognized and understood by their funders and donors, financiers and patrons, and if this space of acknowledgement and humility is nurtured at a consortium level, it would not threaten leaders and organizations to be petrified of the witch hunt in the face of disclosure of some transgression within the organization or by the spouse or children of the leadership.

10

MORALITY AND JUDGEMENTS OF ICC MEMBERS

Personal moralities

extra-marital relationships

ICC biases

moral judgments

Anand was on his way to an important meeting. As the financial controller of Busch Bank, he had an important presentation to make today and was going through his notes when someone suddenly touched his arm. 'Hi', said Keerti. In her late 20s, Keerti was the deputy head of corporate social responsibility (CSR) in the bank and a real go-getter. She had joined the bank about three years earlier and had quickly moved up the ranks. Anand and she had worked together on some large-scale CSR initiatives, and they had swiftly developed a close friendship.

Anand was in his late 30s, happily married with two young boys. His wife, Ferhana, was a stay-at-home mom, who was devoted to her children as well as to her workaholic husband. Anand had been promoted to financial controller at a relatively young age and worked 70-hour weeks to prove (mostly to himself) that he was worthy of his senior position. His wife was fully supportive of his passion and drive and swallowed her own loneliness and frustration, telling herself that Anand was working so hard out of love for her and their family.

Anand and Keerti had met initially when Keerti had joined the bank, as they had been asked to work together on some rural healthcare projects for the CSR department. Since the bank had never ventured into rural healthcare before, the project involved putting in long hours as well as a lot of innovation and brainstorming. Both Anand and Keerti, desperate to prove their worth, had dived into the project headfirst, eating, sleeping and breathing work. They had had to spend hours and hours together, and as expected, became fast friends. Anand respected Keerti's maturity that belied her young age, and Keerti was in awe of Anand's ability to juggle all of his professional responsibilities and still find time to relax and have fun with colleagues. They shared the same sense of humour and keen ambition and realized that they made a formidable team.

After the success of the first project they did together, Anand and Keerti were given several more opportunities to work together on completely revamping the way Busch Bank approached its CSR initiatives, over the next year. They thoroughly enjoyed working together, and their friendship blossomed into intimacy. Anand found himself looking forward to meeting Keerti at the end of a busy day, not just to talk shop but to generally spend time with her. Keerti also felt a strange pull towards this man, who was quite a bit older than her, but who had a gift for making her feel valued and cared for.

The financial controller of the bank, Ashwin, spotted it before either Anand or Keerti did. As a good friend of Anand's, the two men used to make it a point to go out for a drink once a week, just to relax and catch up on each other's lives. One day, when they were at their usual bar, Ashwin decided to confront Anand. 'So tell me, man. What's going on with you and that girl, Keerti?' he asked directly. Anand was surprised. 'What do you mean? We're friends, dude and we work together a lot', he said. 'What rubbish, *yaar.* I have seen the way you look at each other', responded Ashwin with a smile. 'You can't tell me that nothing's going on!' Anand looked surprised and just shook his head, to which Ashwin said 'Okay, if you say so, but I'm just telling you man, be careful. You're playing with fire if Ferhana finds out.'

Anand just rolled his eyes at his friend and didn't think about the conversation until the next time he met Keerti, which was the following week. He had been super busy with some other work but had found himself thinking about Keerti a lot, wondering what she was up to and wondering whether to text her. 'Stupid Ashwin', he thought to himself. 'Putting thoughts in my head that weren't even there earlier!' He finally didn't text Keerti and when she touched his arm in the hallway, pulling him out of his reverie, he was startled. 'How are you, Anand? Been a while', she said, smiling at him. 'Shall we catch up soon?'

They made plans to go out for dinner that evening and Anand called Ferhana to tell her that he had to work late and to not make dinner for him. He felt a mild pinch of guilt, which faded away as soon as he saw Keerti in the restaurant. They had a wonderful time, after which they started meeting often for dinner, drinks or just to chat. Anand always felt guilty telling his wife that he had to work late but she was so used to it by now that she didn't mind, which made him feel better, in some strange way.

A year passed. Anand and Keerti continued to do well in the organization and continued to spend more and more time with each other as the months passed. Ashwin's initial suspicions about their relationship became true, with both Anand and Keerti finally realizing that they had feelings for each other. They briefly tried to stay away from each other but to no avail. Anand realized that in spite of being happily married, he had fallen irrevocably in love with his colleague. Keerti, in turn, made it very clear to him that his marriage didn't mean anything to her since she had really strong feelings for him, unlike any man she had ever met.

Almost without realizing it, Anand and Keerti's relationship developed and deepened into a full-blown affair. They spent nights together, went on weekend getaways together and their relationship became obvious to everyone who saw them around each other at the office. They had many intimate conversations about the future, with Anand telling Keerti that he couldn't live without her and that he'd find a way to make it work, long-term. Keerti reassured him saying that marriage wasn't on the cards for her, at least for the next couple of years, but they still made plans of where they'd live, travel and how many kids they'd have after marriage. Keerti found herself thinking about their life together and wondering when Anand would finally separate from his wife.

Anand found himself thinking about his wife as well, and the life they shared with their two boys. Even though he had fallen deeply in love with Keerti, Ferhana was an amazing wife, nurturer and a wonderful mother to their sons. He grappled with the dilemma of his double life but let things stay as they were. 'Why fix something that isn't broken?' he thought to himself. His lives with Keerti and Ferhana were separate, and he was happy both at work and at home. He felt that as long as he was being a good partner to both these women, he wasn't hurting anyone. 'Let me think about marriage later', he told himself, since Keerti wasn't keen on it at the moment and just continued on with life looking very much like before.

One day, everything changed. Anand was in a team meeting in a conference room when he heard loud screams and noises outside. He immediately ran to the hallway where, to his shock, he saw Ferhana, with tears streaming down her cheeks, shouting at Keerti. 'You home-wrecker! Do you have any idea what you've done?' he heard her scream. 'You've ruined my life!' she shouted, swinging her bag at Keerti, hitting her with it hard. Keerti, who was clearly on her way to a meeting, seemed to be paralysed from shock and could only stand in one place, holding a stack of files while Ferhana repeatedly hit her with her bag. The cries of 'slut' and 'home-wrecker' finally alerted security, who had to physically restrain Ferhana and escort her from the building. Anand, with his heart hammering, had not intervened at all. In fact, seeing the two women together had hit him so hard that he found himself leaving office early that day. Realizing that he could not face Ferhana at home, he had driven around aimlessly for hours, finally deciding to stay at a hotel for the night and go directly to work the next day.

Rumours followed Anand around at work for the next few days. It was whispered that another senior executive's wife had somehow found out about Anand and Keerti's affair and had told Anand's wife about it. Another rumour went around that Keerti herself had orchestrated the entire thing; sick of Anand's inability to leave his wife and commit to her, she had texted Ferhana about the affair. Anand was in a daze. All he knew was that he had to somehow win Ferhana back and save his family. His boys' faces kept surfacing in his mind, and he realized that he would have to go back home sometime, to face the music and make things right.

Making things right was easier said than done. Anand could simply not summon up the courage to face his wife. After a week of staying at a hotel, Anand finally got a call from Ferhana's father, who demanded that he go back home and talk to her. He numbly did what he was told and after going home, realized that Ferhana had told his parents as well as her own parents about the affair and that everyone had descended on the house. His parents had come down to visit because Ferhana's parents were threatening to file a cruelty case against him, for his adultery and his neglect of their daughter and their grand children. After several days of tears and drama, Anand and Ferhana finally agreed to see a couples' counsellor and to stay together, for the time being. She and her family had two conditions: Anand was to come home directly after work every single day, and he was to completely stop seeing Keerti for good.

Anand abruptly cut Keerti out of his life. He stopped returning her calls, responding to her messages and started actively avoiding her at work. His superiors had already heard the rumours, and after seeing the public spat between Ferhana and Keerti in the office, had issued him stern warnings about acceptable office conduct. They did not work together anymore, as he had requested to be removed from all of her projects. After a few months, Anand slowly felt like things were getting better. He had heard, through the company grapevine, that Keerti was doing well in her new projects and he felt that couples' counselling was also going relatively well with Ferhana. 'I am finally getting my life back', he told Ashwin. 'I made a huge mistake and I feel so relieved that this is all over.'

Little did Anand know that his troubles were far from over. About two months after Ferhana found out about his affair, Anand was summoned by the head of HR to be told that Keerti had filed sexual harassment proceedings against him, admitting to their entire affair. In her complaint, she had said that their entire affair and the sexual relationship was consensual but said that it had been 'incumbent on a promise of marriage'. She said that because Anand would clearly never marry her, their entire affair had been without her informed consent. She accused Anand of sexual harassment over the span of their year-old relationship.

Anand was horrified. In almost a daze, he approached a lawyer and submitted a hastily written defence to the company. He tried to say that the entire relationship was consensual and had nothing to do with either his or Keerti's professional life. In his hearing before the five-member ICC, he stressed on consent, saying that he had no intent to sexually harass Keerti and admitting to being in love with her. He argued his own case for more than an hour, leaving him emotionally spent and exhausted.

After Anand's hearing, the ICC members decided to hold an internal meeting. The ICC consisted of a chairwoman, Payal Rohatgi, three senior-level female employees and Dr Anita Parth, the founding member of a prominent women's rights non-profit organization. They all met at a conference room and started to discuss the case.

After some time, the members realized that they were deeply divided with some members accusing Anand of manipulation and abuse of power, and some finding him absolutely innocent. One of the senior-level employees, Swati Manchanda, argued vehemently that Anand was a master manipulator. 'Look at the facts', she said. 'This is a senior-level employee who's been with the bank for years. He clearly knew what he was doing when he got himself allocated to the same projects as the victim. He also told her that they would get married, leading her on for years! If that's not manipulation, I don't know what is', she concluded firmly. Shruti Kumar, a senior accounts manager, disagreed.

'Firstly, he never promised her marriage', she said. 'By all accounts, he was completely open with her about being married with children, and the victim never had a problem with it. They've been having an affair for more than a year, and suddenly, she files a complaint? I think that if there is manipulation, it's arguably from her side', she said.

Dr Anita was not convinced by either person's perspective. 'Frankly, I am surprised that things were allowed to escalate this much', she said. 'Anand is a senior employee who had a very public affair with a junior-level employee. Everyone in their departments knew what was going on. Did he not stop to think that his behaviour was highly unprofessional?' she asked, incredulously. Nobody responded for a few minutes and then the chairwoman spoke up. 'You're right, Anita', she said. 'As a senior employee who represents the bank in various international fora, Anand had a responsibility to know the boundaries of appropriateness. What he did was exceedingly unprofessional, and I don't think we should tolerate such behaviour.'

'I agree that it was unprofessional, Ms Rohatgi', said Sanjana Reddy, the deputy head of sales. 'But was it actually sexual harassment? That's what we are concerned with, isn't it? Even if Anand knowingly violated boundaries and acted inappropriately with a colleague, he never acted against her will or without her consent.' 'She only gave her consent because he promised her a future', said Swati. 'If he had told her that he was just using her, which he obviously was, she would never have had a relationship with him.'

After some deep thought, Payal Rohatgi nodded. 'He knew exactly what he was doing', she said, with finality. 'He had a responsibility towards the organization to act professionally, and his affair led to a very public scene, which makes the bank look really bad', she sighed. 'Anand showed clear interest in the complainant, manipulated her into having a sexual relationship with him and violated professional boundaries for over a year. I see no doubt in what we have to do.' She looked at the others. 'Let's put it to a vote.'

A month later, Keerti was walking into her office when she heard two people talking, just behind the door. She recognized them as her colleagues, Sanjana and Alex. 'Keerti's ruined his career', Sanjana said. 'After the ICC found him guilty, senior management suspended him, and I heard from Vanitha in HR yesterday that he's been fired. All for a consensual relationship', she scoffed.

'Yeah, well, are you surprised?' said Alex. 'The ICC is filled with those middle-aged women, what did you think they were going to say to this case? Obviously, any public affair was going to scandalize them! Also, I heard that this Keerti had talked in detail about their sex life in her complaint, so for sure these aunties would have been shocked.'

'You're right', agreed Sanjana. 'They were bound to get all moral after reading that he slept with her. Imagine if he had not slept with her, would that have been considered sexual harassment?'

'I really don't know', replied Alex. 'They obviously thought he manipulated her, and the fact that he got her to sleep with him would have probably convinced them that she was a victim. Also, it's all about optics, right?' he added. 'There was such a bad scene with his wife coming and screaming at Keerti in front of everyone in the office. I heard that even the finance director saw it! There's no way the bank could have let that go.'

'Yeah, for sure', agreed Sanjana. 'If he had done this maybe five years later, they'd never have sacked him. They needed to set an example, and he was the perfect guy to use to prove a larger point. While he was in a senior position, he was not indispensable to the organization—and that makes all the difference.'

Over the last couple of decades, there have been increasing numbers of cases wherein women have charged men with rape on grounds of deceit and fraud for having had sex with them with promises of marriage. And on several such cases, the courts have decided that complainants can accuse them of fraud and cheating but not rape. Similarly, in this case, the ICC members could easily concur that it was inappropriate and unprofessional of Anand to have engaged in an extramarital affair with a junior colleague with little heed to the implications on the organization and the impact of the affair on the office. What seemed to be a point of disagreement, especially with Shruti and Sanjana, was whether this extends to sexual harassment and can Keerti claim to be the victim of his manipulation without taking responsibility for having engaged in an affair with him while he was married.

The deliberation of the ICC members reflects their personal moralities around extramarital affairs, reduced responsibility of the younger woman and greater onus of the older man, who is also professionally senior to her. Dr Anita's question on whether the company should have tolerated such an affair that was no secret to anyone also reveals her disapproval of the affair itself. No one made any mention of HR policies on office romance and relationships, and if the affair was so public, then either Anand was oblivious of any such policy, nor did Ashwin or the HR make any mention of it, throughout the year when they were involved. Even after Ferhana's public confrontation with Keerti, HR did not call for any meeting to address what had become an organizational issue.

As expected, scars of such incidents create more mistrust and anger in the system which leaks in corridor gossip. Unless such matters are dealt with sensitivity and transparency, it is likely to leave various kinds of residue amongst other employees. The case also reveals how, without adequate training of ICC members, it may end up operating completely from personal moral judgements than from an organizational policy and its principles.

11

LOVE, POWER AND PATRIARCHY

Appropriateness

workplace boundaries

preconceived patriarchal notions

gender neutrality

culture-building

in the workplace. Workplace affairs and romances between married and unmarried individuals have been on the rise and different organizations handle this development differently.

One HR professional talked about how their IT organization discourages office relationships and mandates that employees disclose their relationships to the company, whereas another HR professional said that her company did not have any strict policies. Employees could enter into relationships with each other if they chose and she said that many marriages took place as well, between colleagues. Moral judgements around office relationships and marriage can dictate outcomes of sexual harassment complaints, illustrated by Anand and Keerti's story in chapter 10. Although the POSH committee was found to be in Keerti's favour, saying that she was 'manipulated' by her successful, older, married boss, her colleagues felt sorry for Anand, labelling Keerti as 'manipulative' for complaining about what they saw as a consensual relationship between two adults.

EXTERNAL FACTORS

Cultural idioms on masculinities as well as feminineness also play a direct link between what can be deemed 'appropriate' behaviour in the workplace. For instance, one senior-level employee from a multinational corporation (MNC) had said that in their organization, there were several instances where women who complained about sexual harassment by their male colleagues actually had no problem with the behaviour of their colleagues but had filed the harassment complaint upon the insistence of their husbands, who found the 'familiarity' exhibited by the male colleague to be wholly inappropriate. She recounted one such POSH committee hearing, where the complainant actually said, 'I have no issue with how he behaved (referring to the accused) but my husband said it is unacceptable for him to call me after 10 PM and said I must file a complaint.'

The above narrative shows the direct link between ideals of masculinity, aggression, power and appropriateness—where the husband of the complainant was not the actual victim of sexual harassment but sought to reclaim his power from the 'other man', who had supposedly behaved inappropriately or in an 'over-friendly' manner with his wife. Further, as Mannan's story shows that ideals of masculinity, often, don't contemplate victimization. Even though Mannan may very well have been sexually harassed, his masculinity, as well as the femininity of his 'harasser' led him to dissociate from victimhood to the point where even when he was confronted, he denied that he was ever a victim.

PRECONCEIVED PATRIARCHAL NOTIONS

The notion that men are automatically perpetrators and women are, by default, victims, is seen in many organizations and rests firmly on gender stereotypes and heteronormativity. This notion also finds a place in law, which provides recourse for sexual harassment of 'women' in the workplace—notably excluding men—as well as persons who do not subscribe to the gender binary. This begs the question as to how organizations can formulate inclusive policies for people of different sexual identities and orientations and deal with issues of safety, discrimination and fairness, taking into account conflicts and dilemmas that may arise. Naresh's story in Chapter 8, explored prejudice, homophobia and illegality when it came to 'homosexuality in the workplace', showing that many organizations are wholly unequipped to even understand alternative sexualities, equating them with deviance and perversion. For Naresh, a gay man who confessed to his boss that he was being discriminated because of his sexuality, he received no closure, consolation nor resolution. After leaving the company and going back to his hometown, he was left with the question—did I experience sexual harassment? Is harassment and discrimination on account of my sexuality something that can come under 'sexual harassment'? Without any organizational policy on the same, his guess is as good as ours.

We have seen that we cannot disassociate our bodies and genders from any engagement between people in an organization. In spite of gender playing such a huge role in determining 'appropriateness', it is often a stated belief that in order to create professional workplaces one must be valued for one's skills and competencies, dedication and sincerity, values and ethics and not on the basis of one's gender or sexual identity. This begs the question, what does gender neutrality mean in such a context? And what does 'professionalism' mean without acknowledging gender identities? Organizational systems end up creating splits between espoused values on gender and sexuality and values in action. Let us take the example of the HR professional who talked about how workplace relationships were discouraged in her IT company and those employees would have to mandatorily disclose such relationships. In such a case, the organization's espoused value was that of 'professionalism', where people would be expected to treat each other as neutered entities, to be engaged with only on a professional level, ignoring gender identities, attractions, tensions and sexualities. In spite of these espoused values, the HR professional recounted instances where people felt attracted towards each other and sometimes even got married while being the subject of gossip in the organization.

The dichotomy between espoused values and values in action is clearly seen in non-profits, as seen by the stories of Anisha Ratnam and Womxn First in Chapter 9. While many non-profits that work on gender violence, sexual harassment and women's rights are vocally moralistic, their own employees often undergo tumultuous relationships with each other with some ending up in marriage, some going through civil or messy breakups and some having very public extramarital affairs. In the absence of a larger conversation around organizational culture and appropriateness within the non-profits, the values in action are dealt through turning a blind eye to contradictions, or through gossip, which is the system's way of dealing with conflicts through shame and guilt.

ABUSE OF POWER

We have also attempted to deal with issues of abuse of power, and we find that in almost all of our stories, there is an inherent 'power' component that can dictate whether employees feel like they have been sexually harassed, whether complaints are made, the perceptions and conversations around relationships and harassment and the actual outcomes of sexual harassment complaints. Whether we talk about Anand and Keerti's story, where their colleagues opined that if the complaint had been made five years later, Anand would not have been fired; or Rajeev and Malini's story (Chapter 1), where Rajeev's seniority made his flirtations and pursuit of, Malini even more forceful there needs to be a larger conversation on the intersectionality of power, hierarchy and sexuality in a workplace. Organizations should aim at making people more aware of how sexuality, power, hierarchy and authority get played out in a working system. That dialogue and awareness would diffuse unstated tensions and empower a system and its members to build stronger interpersonal relationships, co-hold boundaries between the self and role in a workplace more effectively.

A multitude of factors that impact and characterize interpersonal relationships and standards of behaviour in the workplace need to be tackled in more nuanced ways than simply 'banning' certain kinds of relationships and threatening punishment for perpetrators. Although a POSH committee is an extremely important and mandatory structure in a workplace, organizations need to have larger conversations around culture, trust and comfort-building amongst their employees. This cannot happen in a day, but it has to be subject to target initiatives over a substantial period of time. In today's day and age, where technology and society have become inalienably interconnected, organizations can reach out to their employees through videos and other online techniques. One organization that approached the lead author for advice about culture-building said that they had a cafeteria where all the employees would gather at lunchtime, where there was a large television. Upon the author's suggestion, they started using the space to show videos that talked about 'appropriateness' and 'inappropriateness' to their employees. They did not prescribe any black and white standards of what is appropriate and not, instead talked about how appropriateness is subjective. Through visual examples, they showed that you decide what is appropriate behaviour for you, which can differ from other people. Through their videos, they showed their employees that being able to communicate openly with their colleagues was a mark of trust and not mistrust, encouraging dialogue and conversation around people's boundaries and notions of acceptability.

The organization then put in place an 'employee engagement service'. After playing their videos, they undertook a qualitative analysis to see people's perceptions of how they received and perceived the content. This was helpful for them to understand where employees stood and the initiatives to put in place to take their 'gender and diversity' programme forward. It helped them to understand the diversity within the organization and to improve interpersonal communication.

Topics like 'jokes' were addressed as there can be a thin line between jokes and offensive statements with a cardinal principle being set, which is that a statement is either a joke or offensive, depending upon the perception of the receiver. The topic of 'political correctness' was also addressed, as such policies may be seen to 'stifle' the expression of some people and identities within the organization.

AN INCLUSIVE AND EVOLVING ORGANIZATIONAL CULTURE

Although there is no sure-fire method to 'eliminate' sexual harassment in any organization, encouraging open communication, conversations and awareness on gender identity, diversity and subjective standards of appropriateness and inappropriateness must be a priority. Perceptions around such open communication should be that they are important for trust and comfort-building, allowing for differing viewpoints and unintended consequences.

Building an organizational culture is something that must come from within the organization, rather than be treated as a top-down approach, where values are likely to be imposed rather than acquired. Alternative, non-heterosexual, non-binary and marginalized identities must be acknowledged, with all their vulnerabilities and sensitivities. Finally, the aim of all of these conversations and initiatives is to gradually build a consensus in any system, which is defined by the people within the system. An inclusive, open and evolving organizational culture is the first step towards improving safety, inclusivity and participation in any workplace.

12

QUID PRO QUO

transactional sex

casting couch

quid pro quo

perpetrator impunity

celebrity transgressions

MeToo

systemic responses to harassment

Narratives of sexual harassment, safety, gender diversity and power from people in different sectors may reflect unique individual experiences but, invariably, show some common patterns. These patterns run through various sectors including but not limited to the media and entertainment industry, the corporate sector, the unorganized workplace and the non-profit sector. This chapter will attempt to explore a few of the more pervasive patterns that we see and suggest a framework that can be adopted across workplaces to address and avoid these patterns.

One common pattern that is seen is the 'quid pro quo' narrative that characterizes many interactions between survivors of sexual harassment and abusers, where sexual favours are exchanged for some opportunity or benefit. In the entertainment industry, for instance, the 'casting couch' is a reality, where aspiring actresses—or even actors—perform sexual favours for directors, producers or other people in power, after being promised that if they do so, they will be cast in movies, TV shows and receive other major opportunities coveted by many. People who demand sexual favours in exchange for such opportunities (the abusers or accused) often seek to justify or rationalize their actions, stating that they don't 'force' anybody to perform sexual favours and that whoever comes to them does so entirely at their own discretion and will.

Further, the 'quid pro quo' narrative also comes with a common bystander response. Given that the majority of instances of sexual harassment and sexual activity are demanded by men from women, bystanders commonly respond to reports of sexual harassment, or 'casting couch' in the entertainment industry, by casting responsibility on the woman. While bystanders acknowledge that people who demand sexual favours do exist in the industry, they state that nobody 'forces' anyone to perform sexual favours for them. Many women from the Indian film industry, for instance, when asked about their struggles with opportunity and success, state proudly that they had come across the casting couch in the industry but 'did not compromise'. They were also clear that 'nobody forces you' to do anything you do not want to do and that it is a transaction of sorts, with a clear benefit for the woman. Famous Bollywood choreographer, Saroj Khan, made one such statement regarding the casting couch in Bollywood. Her exact words translated into English were: 'This has been going on for ages. Everybody wants to try on a girl, even the government employees. Why are you after the film industry? At least they provide a livelihood. They don't leave someone after raping them.' Thereafter, she continued by stating: 'It is up to the girl as to what she wants to do. If you don't want to give in, you won't. If you have the skills and art, why would you sell yourself? Don't say anything about the film industry, they are our godfather'.[1]

Saroj Khan's comments summarize the predominant view taken with respect to the 'quid pro quo' narrative, as a bystander. Although she received flak for her statement and subsequently issued an apology, she also received support from actor Richa Chadha, who accused everyone else of overreacting and unfairly targeting the Indian film industry,

---

[1] Sampada Sharma, 'Saroj Khan Defends Casting Couch in Bollywood, Says It at Least Provides Livelihood,' *Indian Express*, 24 April 2018. Available at: https://indianexpress.com/article/entertainment/bollywood/saroj-khan-casting-couch-5149516/ (accessed on 10 August 2020).

when such incidents 'takes place in all industries'.[2] Therefore, the commonality of sexual harassment is acknowledged, but consent is constructed in such a way that the act of asking for sexual favours seems to be completely not judged.

The socialization of sexual privilege clearly intertwines with power, where people in positions of power are free to exercise their sexual privilege, without judgement. The onus of engaging in sexual activities with a 'quid pro quo' narrative is placed entirely on the woman in the situation, or the 'heroine', if we consider the entertainment industry. Typically, the heroine is a girl or a woman in her late teens or 20s, whereas the accused and offenders are older men, who could be producers, directors, actors or agents. The pattern we see is that even when people talk about the casting couch and exchanging sexual favours for opportunities *post facto*, there are no names mentioned. Therefore, we see that there is a high level of impunity here.

Impunity of sexual harassers can be seen in three patterns. First, impunity occurs because of the widespread normalization of predatory behaviour. Common narratives around the 'big, bad world' acknowledge that 'men will ask/ demand sexual favours' and turn the onus onto the vulnerable victim, with instructions that she should be strong and never 'fall for' such advances or demands. This situation can be transposed into a number of settings with a similar pattern in corporate workplaces—as seen in some of our stories earlier in this book—or even in daily life, where mothers tell their daughters that men are predatory and that they have to take their own precautions to stay safe. Many people truly

---

[2] ANI,'Casting Couch Row: Richa Chadha Comes out in Support of Choreographer,' *Deccan Chronicle,* 25 April 2018. Available at: https://www.deccanchronicle.com/entertainment/bollywood/250418/saroj-khan-casting-couch-row-richa-chadha-comes-out-in-support.html (accessed on 10 August 2020).

believe that asking for sexual favours is different from raping someone, which calls for defining predatory behaviour and calling it out as a violation, abnormal.

Second, impunity occurs because of untold fears of the victims or bystanders, where they are afraid of disclosing what they went through or witnessed. One reason that allowed the #MeToo campaign to take place in the Indian film industry is that none of the top stars of the industry spoke up, nor faced accusations of sexual misconduct. One incident that was repeatedly covered in the #MeToo movement was about prominent actress, Rekha, who was forcibly kissed by actor Biswajit on the sets of a film when she was 15 years old, in the presence of multiple witnesses. The incident was brought to light in a book, *Rekha: The Untold Story*,[3] by writer Yasser Usman, but till date, Rekha has not spoken about it at all. Further, top film actors and leading industry professionals were notably left out of any accusations, showing how insulated they can be from the #MeToo discourse.

The overwhelming silence of many women, some of whom were subjected to sexual harassment or assault for many years prior to them coming out, like in the Bernie Sanders case,[4] may seem like collusion with abusers or accused in an oppressive system but actually shows the fear of confrontation and stigma that survivors experience. Whether we talk about the multiple allegations against Harvey Weinstein[5] or Bernie

---

[3] Yasser Usman, *Rekha: The Untold Story* (New Delhi: Juggernaut Books, 2016)

[4] A series of sexual harassment allegations were made against top male campaign staffers working on Bernie Sanders' 2016 presidential campaign. More information at: Sydney Ember and Katie Benner, 'Sexism Claims from Bernie Sanders's 2016 Run: Paid Less, Treated Worse,' *New York Times*, 2 January 2019. Available at: https://www.nytimes.com/2019/01/02/us/politics/bernie-sanders-campaign-sexism.html (accessed on 10 August 2020).

[5] 'Harvey Weinstein Timeline: How the Scandal Unfolded,' *BBC News*, 29 May 2020. Available at: https://www.bbc.com/news/entertainment-arts-41594672 (accessed on 10 August 2020)

Sanders's campaign staff,[6] there is no way to anticipate an 'outcome' of the allegations, given these individuals' immense power and influence. The first few women who called out Harvey Weinstein for sexual misconduct presumably had no idea that their statements would lead to a string of disclosures by other women and had no way of knowing the outcomes or fallout of their allegations. The Harvey Weinstein case ultimately snowballed into a movement, simply because people were angry and willing to talk about their experiences from the past. One reason for the silence that lasted so many years was a lack of faith in the system. The possibilities of facing stigma and loss of work create an untold fear in survivors of sexual harassment and abuse, which may be well-founded. For instance, the actor Parvathy, who took on Malayalam film stalwarts Mammootty and Mohanlal, over issues relating to misogyny in movies to 'shielding' the actor Dileep in the Association of Malayalam Movie Artists (AMMA) after he was accused in a conspiracy to rape another actor.[7] She experienced significant fallout after her statements, in the form of cyberbullying, rape and death threats.[8] She additionally experienced trouble with work, stating that 'people find it difficult to work with a whistle-blower'.[9]

---

[6] Ember and Benner, 'Sexism Claims.'

[7] 'Parvathy Speaks out Against Misogyny in Films Like Kasaba, Gets Trolled by Mammootty Fans,' *Hindustan Times*, 13 December 2017. Available at: https://www.hindustantimes.com/regional-movies/parvathy-speaks-out-against-misogyny-in-films-like-kasaba-gets-trolled-by-mammootty-fans/story-os3EK9TsSmYZV4YYwSGutO.html (accessed on 10 August 2020).

[8] Gautaman Bhaskaran, 'Mammootty's Fans are Sending Parvathy Rape and Death Threats. Shame on Him,' Daily O, 20 December 2017. Available at: https://www.dailyo.in/arts/parvathy-trolled-mammootty-kasba-vijay-dileep-online-abuse/story/1/21271.html (accessed on 10 August 2020).

[9] Manu Balachandran, 'Parvathy: The Activist Star,' *Forbes India*, 11 December 2018. Available at: https://www.forbesindia.com/article/2018-celebrity-100/parvathy-the-activist-star/52013/1 (accessed on 10 August 2020).

The #MeToo movement, while revolutionary in many ways, has become the subject of 'jokes' now, with people showing their large-scale denial of the seriousness of sexual harassment by making light of the movement and underlying culture of toxic patriarchy, impunity and silence, resulting in the sexual harassment. The more powerful the people, the less likely they are to engage in risk-taking behaviour by openly talking about the issue of sexual harassment in the workplace on a public scale.

The third pattern showing the impunity of sexual harassers comes from bystanders' views and how systems deal with harassment. When the #MeToo movement came to the Indian film industry, the silence of the Ministry of Women and Child Development through Smriti Irani, a notoriously vocal politician, was telling. Smriti Irani was hitherto in the intersection of politics and movies but chose to remain silent right up till the allegations against M. J. Akbar, which forced senior politicians to abandon their facades of neutrality and actually pay attention to the issue.[10] Further, in West Bengal, where many politicians are erstwhile movie stars, there have been no political statements on sexual harassment. Systemically, in workplaces, allegations of sexual harassment and misconduct lead to 'slinging matches' between perpetrators and victims, where some people believe one side and others believe the other side. There is no systemic response but many individual responses and uncanny silence from the leadership.

Although the focus has been on the media and entertainment industry so far, even with corporate sector disclosures like in the cases of Tarun Tejpal and M. J. Akbar, the pattern

[10] Prarthana Mitra, 'Lip Service, Denial and Silence: How Indian Politicians Reacted to #MeToo,' *Qrius*, 20 October 2018. Available at: https://qrius.com/lip-service-denial-and-silence-how-indian-politicians-reacted-to-metoo/ (accessed on 10 August 2020).

remains that the perpetrators are older, powerful men and the victims have been typically younger, junior women. In the entire narrative of sexual harassment, there is very little talk around the role of corporate leadership. Assuming that there were no ICCs, Vishakha Guidelines or sexual harassment legislation, we can see clearly the absence of corporate leadership with a view to culture-building. We have not heard any statements from the Tatas, Ambanis, Nilekani or even Azim Premji and we see that leadership is maintaining its strange silence due to, perhaps, a misguided notion that this is not a matter for corporate leadership to take a stance on. Although organizations have created policies against sexual harassment, there has been no investment in research, no large-scale studies on how to deal with this issue in the workplace and no engagement on 'grey' issues.

Further, in the course of writing this book, none of our several interviewees consented to be named, implying that sexual harassment, violence and power dynamics in the workplace are still not being engaged with openly. One interviewee who was the former head of the ICC of a large financial services company talked about how the ICC members had found themselves 'out of their depth' when dealing with one particularly complex case of sexual harassment. While the ICC members seemed to be qualified people with good intentions, they clearly needed more expertise and help than that offered by the composition. To a certain extent, ICCs and sexual harassment laws have become a 'necessary evil' that form a mandatory part of a compliance checklist in workplaces, especially corporate workplaces. Although companies can be held accountable for not having ICCs, the legal mandate has not induced any rigour in engagement amongst leadership in terms of sexual harassment.

Societal discomfort around sexuality and gender is one of the primary causes for leaders to remain disengaged from sexual harassment and culture-building. Many companies are upfront about queer-friendly policies they have adopted or LGBTQ support groups in the organization. Several such organizations have emerged in the past couple of years, resulting in the image creation of a 'progressive' organization. At this stage, there should be an inquiry or curiosity into delving into what it would mean to work in places with different genders and sexes, where questions around safety, dynamics, power and other issues must be engaged with. One reason that the so-called 'progressive' organizations are not, is because the lens through which sexual harassment is engaged with (the ICC and sexual harassment legislation) is in itself, retributive in nature. Sexual harassment is, therefore, engaged within terms of punishment, rather than forward progression.

When we look at the informal sector, the situation becomes even more complex. At the time of #MeToo, there was a surprising silence from people in the unorganized sector including domestic workers, brick kiln workers and even people who worked in massage parlours. The human rights activist, Sunitha Krishnan, brought this up during the #MeToo movement saying, 'The voices of those who have experienced some of the worst abuse—trafficking victims—have not been heard.' The uncanny silence of the informal sector and the dominance of a narrative that evidence privilege has led to a 'class divide' in how we look at sexual harassment and exploitation of women, in women from different 'class' sections. Routine stories of sexual abuse amongst domestic workers, research studies on trafficked girls and the sexual abuse they face, reports of sexual abuse of girls in massage parlours that act as fronts for brothels; all show that these crimes are overwhelmingly common and all of them hinge on lack of consent of the girls and women involved. In the face of these lived experiences, the silence of the unorganized sector in #MeToo was resounding. One speculative reason for this silence could be the uniform normalization of violence, exploitation and predatory behaviour amongst workers in the unorganized sector.

Another pattern in various sectors, whether the media and entertainment industry or the corporate sector, is that of people feeling unfairly targeted when asked to speak on sexual harassment, gender, violence and power in the workplace. Many of the people we interviewed, from corporates for this book asked why the focus was on the corporate sector, urging us instead to focus on sectors such as law enforcement and the entertainment industry. Although #MeToo was largely entertainment industry focused in India, it could have been made more universal if the Department of Women and Child Welfare or the Labour Ministry or some other political leader had decided to come in. Since there has been no conversation in political circles, our understanding and engagement of #MeToo and issues around sexual harassment and safety have been stunted, in a way.

The questions that we should be asking ourselves at this point include—the different kinds of preventive measures that we can take organizationally and systemically (apart from sexual harassment laws and the ICC), how leaders can build consensus, how we can dissect power structures that govern privilege, power and predatory behaviour and, most importantly, what inclusivity and diversity mean in the workplace. There is very little literature around all these issues, with points of view being individual-focused and not systemic in nature. The way we deal with sexual harassment and safety is almost 'witch hunt' driven, rather than with a view to re-examining and exploring organizational cultures and systemic politics.

Our proposition through this book is that, firstly, we need to broaden the question from sexual harassment and sexual harassment laws to talking about diversity, gender and sexuality in the workplace. Thereafter, we need to look into building an 'enabling culture' where people can talk about these issues, which directly stems from leadership taking a stand and leading the initiative of open, honest communication. Thirdly, in order to systematize this discourse so that it transcends the corporate workplace, government bodies and political leaders need to take a position and respond to movements like #MeToo. If we talk about development and corporate growth, markers of 'progress' should not be piecemeal in nature, for instance, looking at only queer or LGBTQ-related policies, but simultaneous and concurrent.

Sexual harassment is much more than the statutory and criminal justice response through the ICC and courts. We have to remember that even before a violation occurs, there are many stages of support and control that can be exercised by the system. We propose a restorative framework with 'high support–high control' that involves a lot of supportive measures to people within the system. In the context of a workplace, employees are encouraged to talk about boundaries, safety and consent. Questions like how to deal with office affairs and colleagues' safety are engaged with and employees take an active role in building organizational culture. Rather than HR prescribing a set of rules to follow, employees can collectively create a common space to discuss these issues, build consensus and move forward together.

Organizational evolution will only take place if organizational policies around diversity, gender and inclusion, the retributive response mechanism (ICC) and active, engaged leadership come together to enable the creation of safe spaces and cultures. We need to expand our treatment of sexual harassment as something to address retributively and focus on system-level changes. Building cultures of safety, diversity and openness can help to diffuse male sexual privilege and structures of patriarchy found in the workplace and in society itself.

13

TAKING ACTION

Problematising sexual harassment

zero tolerance policies

diversity policies

organizational climate v culture

Over the years, organizations have moved towards increasing employee diversity with more employees from different cultures, genders, upbringing and values working together in the same workplace. We have seen a whole continuum of behaviour and attitudes between people in workplaces where mutual attraction, consent, relationships and personal boundaries can get blurred between persons from different genders and people of the same gender. After exploring various stories around gender, diversity, power, sexuality and violence in different kinds of workplaces, the next logical step to be followed by organizations and leaders involves taking action to address these issues.

THE 'PROBLEM' OF SEXUAL HARASSMENT

The first proposed action is related to the 'problem' of sexual harassment. Diversity within organizations and varied power dynamics, gender identity and personal relationships can, as we have seen in this book, create situations of 'sexual harassment'. Organizations see sexual harassment as a 'problem' and in response to a legal mandate, have set up ICCs to receive and adjudicate complaints. We argue that problematizing sexual harassment is actually counterproductive, creating anxiety in the workplace rather than solving underlying issues.

Organizations that respond to increased diversity in employment from a location of 'vigilance' or 'zero tolerance' evoke anxiety in the workplace. ICCs do not evoke any positive feeling or excitement in workplaces with people just hoping that others do not make complaints, looking at ICCs as a 'burden' or a 'necessary evil'. Complaints lead to unpleasant situations, confrontations and an additional mandate for HR, exacerbation of conflict and polarization amongst employees. Instead of looking at sexual harassment as a problem to be solved, these should be considered from a position of inquiry, exploration and discovery, asking questions like what it actually means to close the gender gap at the workplace.

For instance, when carrying out interviews in different organizations, it was seen that many men (usually in positions of power) had implicit problems with the female authority. Now, if someone has grown up in a patriarchal culture (like most of us) where men hold the power and women are subservient, it is reasonable to expect subconsciously different reactions to male and female authority in the workplace. Employees were found to have different expectations for women in positions of authority, expecting their female bosses to be more understanding, compassionate and sensitive than their male counterparts—fitting with the female idiom many people have grown up with.

Even in the non-profit sector, people working with men, women as well as other genders and sexes respond differently when the same statement is made by a male versus a non-male or female. Women are expected to handle leadership and power differently from men, and any deviation from people's preconceived notions will end up flowing through workplace pipelines as gossip, without the system ever engaging with the underlying issues. Therefore, rather than problematizing sexual harassment and interpersonal relationships in workplaces, these issues should be addressed with a spirit of exploration and discovery, with a view to building a positive enabling culture at the workplace. Ideally, employees should be engaged to become aware of their own preconceived notions, biases and feelings so that they can act on them and deeply engage with issues around gender, sexuality and power.

PRECONCEIVED NOTIONS OF SEXUAL HARASSMENT

Second, when we talk about diversity and sexual harassment in the workplace, sexual harassment itself as a violation must be recognized as only a part of the whole piece. Sexual harassment, in terms of what the law says, implicitly identifies women as being more vulnerable than men, implicitly assumes that people in higher ranks are more powerful than others and essentially contemplates a senior male perpetrator and a junior female victim. These notions are too narrow for a modern and diverse workplace. Therefore, work around gender and sexuality should be seen in a larger continuum within the concept of 'diversity'. Issues only get addressed in workplaces in the context of sexual harassment and violence, whereas the views should be broader. Culture-building on diversity within a workplace should be linked with gender and sexuality as factors that implicitly affect interpersonal interaction and relationships.

Third, when we look at the organizational climate versus organization culture, we see that 'climate' is concerned with maintaining a certain quality of the environment at the workplace, whereas 'culture' refers to an individual's experience of working in an organization. Questions and discussions relating to gender and sexuality in organizations are seen to be uncomfortable in many situations because of their primal nature. Reflections on what it means to be a particular gender and how people feel towards other (and the same) genders are personal questions, which are often not even discussed in familial settings and, therefore, may cause discomfort in organizations if such discussions are invoked, invited or encouraged. A climate-focused organization will refrain from initiating such discussions because any kind of disturbance of the organizational climate may manifest in negative feedback and discomfort of employees. However, we argue that engagement in these discussions, although potentially disconcerting for employees, can actually lead to culture-building.

Subjects that are taboo in social and familial spaces require some effort to be effectively taken up in organizations. When carrying out such activity in one organization, a few employees questioned the necessity of 'personal questions'. They stated that they had come to the organization to work, play a role and obtain remuneration for the same and were unable to understand why they were being asked to reflect on how they engage with different genders. The questions even evoked anger in some employees, as they had never engaged with such issues growing up or in their families. However, upon engagement with the questions, the views and implicit biases of many persons were brought to light, moving the organization towards consensus building. Therefore, organizations should focus on culture-building rather than climate-preservation, in order to ensure that employees are able to introspect, reflect, understand their feelings and engage comfortably with issues around gender, sexuality and power.

Fourth, workplaces must engage with the values of an organization around gender and sexuality. For this, the 'normal' standard in the system must be identified. For example, in a large organization like ITC, the 'normal' 50 years ago would have been that if you were a manager, it could be assumed that you were a man. Similarly, if you were a board member, you could be assumed to be a man; if a secretary, definitely a woman. People above the age of 30 were expected to be married, eventually have children and exhibit strong family values. Every organization has a 'normal' image of its employees, which may be different in different types of workplaces like technology companies, BPOs and non-profits. In GenX companies, 'normal' is very different, where people do not talk about their spouses at work, could be migrants, could be on average much younger than other workplaces and where divorce, singlehood and separation are not taboos.

When talking about gender and sexuality in organizations, we have to see what values lie at the 'centre' and which issues are taboo, at the periphery or outside the boundaries. For example, an organization that introduced an LGBTQ inclusion policy globally, including in its India office, would have to account for the fact that up till last year, homosexuality was criminalized and that even now, a large-scale social stigma exists around homosexuality. The difference between core beliefs of organizations and the contents of such policies can cause widespread tension, and therefore, it is important to understand the hierarchy of values in organizations, taboos and stigmas before implementing such policies.

When we talk about organizations around gender, there are certain kinds of people who are immediately seen as power holders, who bear the 'image' or 'look' that one would expect to see in a certain job. This is seen in many sectors, whether we talk about Indian Administrative Services (IAS) officers (physical stature is one of the criteria of selection), hotel management personnel (front-facing officials have a certain physical appearance), guest relations executives (expected to be predominantly women, with pleasant personalities) and others and while there is no explicit harm in these expectations, it is important to see the organization of gender in the system and the respective value of the people within. Certain genders with 'higher' and 'lower' value in the system will show how power gets distributed within the system. The organization of values around sexuality is seen in 'being illegal', where there was clear collusion between India's erstwhile law around homosexuality and the management's attitude. Even now, with decriminalization, there is no way to definitively say that cultural stigmas in organizations against LGBTQ persons will change.

The last approach we propose is inclusion and participation in policymaking, implementation and monitoring in organizations. Top-down or externally imposed policies are rarely effective, invariably resulting in conflicts between the policy itself, group values and individual values in organizations. For instance, a policy mandating that every employee must maintain professional behaviour at all times may not be implemented in reality within an organization. As we have seen in some case studies, sometimes professional relationships evolve into personal relationships, and HR does not intervene because there are either no complaints or work is not impacted by the relationships. Policies and organizational practices can be different, resulting in alienation within the organization that will not foster consensus building. An organization that has practices different from its policies can be said to have deceptive policies in place.

Organizations can take several strategic actions, as elucidated below, for the expansion of the spirit of the organization and the fostering of 'aliveness'.

1. Understanding the prevailing organizational culture around gender and sexuality, through a baseline audit or some kind of an evaluative process.[1] The dissonances and intersectionality between power and gender, power and sexuality and the hierarchy of organizational values must be determined to take stock of where the organization lies at the moment. This should be done periodically, through annual safety audits, qualitative

[1] 'Six Ways to Prevent Harassment in the Workplace,' *Leading Edge Magazine*, 25 April 2018. Available at: http://leadingedgemag.com/lea-global/6-ways-to-prevent-sexual-harassment-in-the-workplace/ (accessed on 10 August 2020).

research, mapping changing perceptions, experiences and culture.[2]

2. Building a resource team within the organization which will be equipped to deal with the internal enquiry, culture-building and issues rather than using the services of external persons who are more likely to 'diagnose' and 'prescribe' rather than deeply engage with issues. Many consultancies in the market that focus on POSH are creating policies and providing training in workplaces. While these activities could build organizational capacity, it is an external input that is finite in nature. The organization should have its own resource pool or core group, consisting of organizational leaders with decision-making capacities, who will be engaged in trying to (a) understand where the organization stands, culturally and (b) what gender, power and sexuality mean in the organization. This should be seen as a leadership action,[3] followed by interventions of different kinds, depending upon leads and outcomes.
3. Broadening the role and identity of the ICC, which is essentially a body that only comes alive after complaints are made, if at all.[4] Organizations can take strategic action to broaden the mandate of the ICC, which can carry out more supportive work and exercise more

---

[2] Leading Edge, 'Six Ways to Prevent Harassment.'

[3] Frank Dobbin and Alexandra Kalev, 'Training Programs and Reporting Systems Won't End Sexual Harassment. Promoting More Women Will,' *Harvard Business Review*,15 November 2017. Available at: https://hbr.org/2017/11/training-programs-and-reporting-systems-wont-end-sexual-harassment-promoting-more-women-will (accessed on 10 August 2020).

[4] Manasi Karthik, 'Lessons from ACJ: Why ICCs Are Inadequate to Deal with Cases of Sexual Harassment,' *The Caravan*, 14 July 2018. Available at: https://caravanmagazine.in/gender-sexuality/lessons-from-acj-icc-inadequate-sexual-harassment (accessed on 10 August 2020).

control in the organization. Receiving and adjudicating complaints could be considered as a part of the activities of the ICC, and it can, for example, determine positions of safety and larger actions to be taken in an organization towards this end. The role of the ICC should not just be burdensome, with it coming alive only when it plays 'judge', identifying guilt or rejecting complaints. An additional mandate could make the members of the ICC come alive to the organization, beyond just their 'vigilante' position. The ICC could look at preventive work and supportive activities, like the capacity building of the core team, referred to above on gender and identity-based work, clarifying outcomes and desired impacts of proposed interventions and carrying out intra-organizational communication programmes.[5]

[5] Karthik, 'Lessons from ACJ.'

14

SEXUAL HARASSMENT LAWS: THE GOOD, THE BAD, THE INADEQUATE

sexual harassment law

gender-specific laws

female victimization

LGBTQIA+ erasure

prevention of harassment

grievance-redressal failure

ICC incompetence

When we look at 'sexual harassment in the workplace' or 'sexual harassment' itself, as a phenomenon, especially in the corporate sphere, there is a tendency to legalize the entire issue, framing it in the context of the workplace's harassment policy (if there is one), which is supposed to be based on the extensive terms provided under the Sexual Harassment of Women at Workplace (Prevention, Prohibition and Redressal) Act, 2013.

For all legal purposes, the Indian law on sexual harassment is a 'good law', being that it covers most of the usual bases by having a wide definition of sexual harassment, calling for the setting up of internal grievance redressal mechanisms in workplaces and detailed inquiry procedures, talking about punishments and penalties and making employee workshops mandatory. Only when the law is put in practice, do we see that sexual harassment itself is not a black and white issue with a fixed definition but a phenomenon with interspersing social, cultural, power-related, relationship-related and of course, gender and sexuality-related factors. Even with full compliance with the law in workplaces, by setting up internal committees and carrying out workshops, we find that incidents of sexual harassment can be a frequent reality in the modern workplace and that somehow, workplaces still find it challenging to respond to many of them. This begs the question, is the law inadequate and, if so, how?

The first point of issue with the sexual harassment law is in its title 'Sexual Harassment of Women at Workplace (Prevention, Prohibition and Redressal) Act, 2013', which itself makes it clear that this is a law that applies to 'women' victims only. Perpetrators of sexual harassment, however, are gender neutral, meaning that technically if a woman allegedly harasses another woman at work, she can be held liable under the sexual harassment law. This has been lauded by some as progressive, since many crimes against women primarily contemplate male perpetrators, lending credence to the stereotypical impression of a harasser (male) and a victim (female). Further, at the time of drafting the law, the possibility of a gender-neutral law was seen to have been brought up, with the debate captured as 'male vs female' with men's rights groups demanding gender neutrality to enable men to make complaints.[1] The Parliamentary Standing Committee later recommended the law to only apply to women as 'women have been at a disadvantaged position and have been discriminated, abused and harassed'.[2] The committee fell back on the ideology that rampant sexual harassment disempowers women, specifically, and recommended a gender-specific law.[3] The overall objective was to increase female workforce participation and ensure that a robust mechanism existed to protect women's employment rights and the committee stated that a 'balanced and well-structured mechanism giving equal opportunity to both the aggrieved woman and respondent with adequate safeguards and checks is unlikely to give any biased protection to women workforce'.[4]

The lack of gender neutrality of the Act may have been enacted keeping in mind the gender binary and historical (and

---

[1] Available at: https://www.prsindia.org/uploads/media/Sexual%20Harassment/SCR%20Protection%20of%20Women.pdf (accessed on 10 August 2020), p. 17.

[2] Ibid., p. 17.

[3] Ibid., p.17

[4] Ibid., p.17.

prevailing) power imbalances between cis-males and females but in spite of being relatively recent, the law has somehow failed to acknowledge the existence and presence of other genders and sexualities in the workplace. Although the law contemplates the offence of sexual harassment in the nature of a 'gendered' offence that is related to the sex of the people involved, there is no recognition of any diversity beyond male, female and heterosexual in its provisions. Lawyers[5] and activists[6] have discussed the implications of the gender-specificity of the sexual harassment law on gender-variant persons and LGBTQ employees who may undergo workplace harassment and have no legal recourse, whatsoever.

In the past decade, India has arguably come a long way, judicially and legally, acknowledging its LGBT population through landmark judgements like the Navtej Singh Johar judgement that 'decriminalized homosexuality' and the National Legal Services Authority (NALSA) judgement in 2014 that affirmed the fundamental rights of transgender individuals. The Supreme Court waxed eloquent, highlighting various instances of discrimination and harassment meted out to persons of these communities, as well as a plethora of international laws and human rights principles, with a view to affirming the need to recognize these persons' rights to equality, non-discrimination and life with dignity.

These judgements could be said to be watershed moments in LGBT rights in the country but over the past several years, it has been seen that there is still much that needs to change in

---

[5] Gaurav Prakash, 'Gender Neutrality and Sexual Harassment Laws in India,' *Ipleaders* (blog), 3 May 2020. Available at: https://blog.ipleaders.in/gender-neutrality-and-sexual-harassment-laws-in-india/ (accessed on 10 August 2020).

[6] Jessamine Mathew, '"Trans"-itioning to Inclusion: Expanding the Ambit of Workplace Sexual Harassment Law,' *The Leaflet*, 4 August 2019. Available at: http://theleaflet.in/trans-itioning-to-inclusion-expanding-the-ambit-of-workplace-sexual-harassment-law/ (accessed on 10 August 2020).

the way that LGBTQIA+ are perceived and treated in many parts of India. Although some parts of the elite, urban India are more accepting of non-heterosexual sexualities, the majority of openly queer India experiences rampant homophobia (and in the case of trans persons, transphobia) that can severely limit their professional and career options. In fact, the Indian LGBT Workplace Survey, 2016, showed that about 40 per cent of people have faced harassment at their place of employment on account of their gender identity/sexual orientation.[7] Studies have also shown that transgender and LBGT persons are still closeted about their sexuality in the workplace for fear of discrimination and more often than not, are ridiculed and discriminated against when they do come out.[8] Transgender persons still find it extremely difficult to find work opportunities due to the abundant transphobia and prejudice that they experience, seen in the low number of trans employees in the mainstream workforce.[9] Transgender persons frequently face structural barriers right from childhood that impact their opportunities, significantly, and are frequent targets of workplace sexual harassment, both in the formal sector as well as the informal sector.

The sexual harassment law in India protects 'aggrieved women' who come under its ambit. Although the Supreme Court judgements contained detailed acknowledgment of the different kinds of harassment and discrimination faced by persons on account of their gender identity and sexual orientation, the same has evidently not translated into 'inclusion' under relevant domestic laws like the Sexual Harassment Act.

---

[7] Akshat Agarwal, 'Pitch Still Queered: The Pioneer,' *Vidhi*, 29August 2019. Available at: https://vidhilegalpolicy.in/2019/08/29/pitch-still-queered-the-pioneer/ (accessed on 10 August 2020).

[8] Ibid.

[9] Mathew, 'Trans'-itioning to Inclusion.'

In its current form, India's sexual harassment law does not hold any space for the experiences of a trans person in a workplace, or for an LGBQIA+ who undergoes harassment. Naresh's story in 'Being Illegal' was a clear illustration of a homosexual person being discriminated against in his workplace based on his sexual orientation, where there was rampant homophobia, no institutional policy on inclusion and ultimately, there was no escape for Naresh from the bullying and discrimination, apart from actually leaving the workplace. It confirms the worst about Indian workplaces, even in the modern day and brings up the inadequacy of the very scope of the law.

The objective of the sexual harassment law is to 'provide protection against sexual harassment of women at workplace and for the prevention and redressal of complaints of sexual harassment and for matters connected therewith or incidental thereto', which is a relatively broad mandate. When we look at 'protection' within the law in the context of the previous discussion on making space for LGBTQIA+ experiences in the workplace, we see that the 'protection of women' is a wholly insufficient mandate for this law to have, when the reality of interpersonal relationships and sexual dynamics in a diverse workplace encompassing different gender identities goes beyond the man-woman binary. Notwithstanding the paternalistic tone of the law that emphasizes the idea of a woman as a thing to be 'protected', the statutory aim of 'protecting' must be extended to persons of marginalized gender identities as well, as it is 'only when a community is afforded equal protection, procedurally and substantively, that they will be empowered to effectively participate in public.'[10]

The next objective of the sexual harassment law is 'prevention' of sexual harassment, as mentioned in the preamble.

---

[10] Ibid.

Defining sexual harassment in practice is a highly subjective process. Something can be interpreted as sexual harassment or not depending upon the people involved, their relationship and identities, sexualities, power dynamics, workplace culture and a variety of other factors that can change from time to time. Therefore, how does one 'prevent' something that keeps changing and evolving? The law fails to answer this question, with the most concrete provision on 'prevention' contained in the prescribed duties of employers to provide safe working environments, put up posters or signs of the consequences of sexual harassment and details of the ICC, organize workshops and awareness programmes for sensitization, etc. The law does not speak much about prevention, leaving the particulars of what is to be done to the employers, for the most part. Notably, the law does not mention what the 'prevention of sexual harassment' entails in principle, leading to wide scope for interpretation and a scattered response amongst employers in terms of prevention initiatives.

The fact that the sexual harassment act mentions 'workshops' as an employer's duty has led to such programmes burgeoning across different kinds of organizations, with separate firms actually being set up with their primary mandate being doing these workshops. Wide variations in workplace types, demographics and cultures have resulted in many different kinds of internal policies around sexual harassment employed by workplaces, including the infamous positions of 'zero tolerance' and 'vigilance' (covered in Chapter 14) that are fundamentally protectionist in nature and somewhat counterintuitively serve to discourage complaints and further cultures of silence. A review of many sexual harassment policies in different organizations, including many of the organizations in the chapters of this book shows for the most part, in conventional corporate workplaces, 'prevention' consists of periodic workshops that broadly discuss what sexual harassment is, the law and infrastructure for redressal set up in the particular workplace. These workshops may use illustrations or presentations, but ultimately, focus on 'sexual harassment' as a discrete phenomenon, without any parallel or pre-existing effort made to discuss and understand diversity, change and sexuality in the workplace. The law on prevention has been restrictive in this regard, given its emphasis on techniques for prevention, rather than defining the scope and context of prevention of sexual harassment.

For 'prevention' of sexual harassment (that is, in itself, a highly subjective experience) to be discussed meaningfully, employers should engage with employees on what it would mean to work in places with differing genders and sexes, discuss safety, dynamics, power and other issues that may arise in a safe space allowing different voices. The law, in its current form, does not engage with the meaning of 'prevention' beyond the few measures suggested for employers. This suggests a gap that can be addressed by developing a principled idea for what 'prevention' should entail; for instance, 'prevention of sexual harassment by creating non-retributive and non-judgemental avenues for engagement with employees regarding sexuality, diversity, gender and sexual harassment with a view towards building a common organizational culture...' and then leaving it to organizations to adopt customized prevention strategies that are best suited to their needs and demographic.

The final aim of the sexual harassment law as contained in the preamble is 'redressal'. This is the subject upon which the law engages in most detail, by outlining a complaints procedure, as well as, by setting up an ICC to hear and decide sexual harassment complaints in the workplace. However, research has shown that organizational grievance systems can have deep-seated flaws, with sexual harassment complainants being more likely to lose their jobs than those who stay silent about such harassment and women complainants in particular being more likely to either quit their jobs, thereafter, or involuntarily lose them. As covered elsewhere in this book, research has clearly indicated that complaints where offenders end up retaining their jobs are likely to result in a hostile work environment being created for the complainant, leading (almost inevitably) to the complainant seeking alternative employment. Further, the grievance redressal mechanisms set up in organizations do little to curtail or tackle existing biases and attitudes around diversity, shown in the fact that than 55 per cent of respondents in a 2018 survey in India, expressed that they still experience bias in their workplaces over factors including gender, ethnicity and sexual orientation.[11]

Questions around grievance redressal in organizations start from the time period prescribed by the law of three months, extendable to six months given to complainants to make complaints of sexual harassment using the company's internal grievance mechanisms. Practicing lawyers have defended the relatively short time frame, stating that three to six months is not a restrictive limitation and pointing out that if the period for complaints was made higher, it would make evidence collection that much more difficult for the grievance redressal system. However, a large number of sexual harassment incidents occur in settings or situations where 'hard evidence' is unlikely to be unearthed, with no video footage, recordings or eyewitnesses and nothing except the word of the victim against that of the accused. The relationship between the time period for a complaint and the quality of evidence

[11] 'India Inc Is Not Creating Inclusive Workplace for LGBT Employees,' *The Economic Times*, 24 November 2018. Available at: https://economictimes.indiatimes.com/news/politics-and-nation/india-inc-is-not-creating-inclusive-workplace-for-lgbt-employees-people-with-disabilities/articleshow/66778071.cms?from=mdr (accessed on 10 August 2020).

that can be unearthed is tenuous, at best and may at most, impact witness testimony or, in the rare case that video footage/ recording exists, allow for it to be used before it is routinely deleted by the company. A significant proportion of sexual harassment incidents, like passing sexually coloured remarks and making physical advances behind closed doors are unlikely to benefit, evidence-wise, from the limitation period of three to six months.

Undergoing harassment at the workplace of any kind can be a deeply traumatic, stressful and isolating experience for any employee, resulting in short and long-term effects on physical and mental health. One complainant, Riddhima, came forward seven months after experiencing three separate non-consensual incidents where her colleague had made physical advances and sexually coloured remarks towards her and filed a complaint before her workplace ICC. She revealed how it had taken her months to actually process what had happened and deal with her own anxiety, fear and trauma before she felt 'ready' to file a formal complaint. The colleague who had allegedly harassed her was an acquaintance who she frequently came across at work, making the process of complaining without fear of professional and personal consequences, very difficult. Further, Riddhima stated that she derived significant stress from even considering the prospect of having to go through the entire inquiry process and 'relive' the entire experience. Riddhima's stress and trauma over the period of time before she made the complaint impacted her work productivity, workplace attitude and output, rendering her belated complaint inadmissible as well as not credible in the eyes of the ICC and senior management. The ICC did not take up the complaint because of the delay and somehow Riddhima's identity, the accused's identity and the details of the harassment were 'leaked' and became fodder for gossip and scandal for the next several months. Although Riddhima stayed in the workplace for two more years out of financial necessity, she said that the incident and response of the ICC permanently affected her interpersonal relationships at the workplace and exacerbated her mental health issues, which she is still recovering from.

The interactions with Riddhima as well as narratives from the #MeToo movement (where thousands of women took to social media to share accounts of being sexually harassed and assaulted) overwhelmingly show that it can take years for survivors to process the trauma that they went through (or were still going through) and speak out about their experiences, or attempt to seek recourse. To, therefore, restrict the time period for complaints to three to six short months, leaving complainants with no redressal beyond India's largely victim-unfriendly criminal justice system, can therefore be counterproductive to creating a safe space for people to be able to share their experiences without fear of dismissal or reprisal. Although the time limit itself is a fairly commonplace statutory clause, the very nature of sexual harassment offences, the trauma they invoke and the emotional labour required to be expended by complainants during the redressal process, all raise questions about the suitability of the limitation period.

Riddhima's narrative on how she felt the need to 'prepare' herself for the ICC proceedings indicates the emotional labour that complainants have to expend to essentially place themselves at the mercy of a jury of their peers, whose responsibility is to find evidence and determine whether harassment has taken place or not. Although the sexual harassment law prescribes the composition of the ICC to include senior level female employees in the workplace, as well as an independent 'expert', reality shows that ICCs rarely have the expertise or competence necessary to fairly adjudicate a sexual harassment complaint. A graphic designer, Zaiba, shared her experience of complaining about sexual harassment by a colleague in her organization. The colleague had sent her several text messages of a sexual nature and had made unwanted physical advances, which spurred her to file an official complaint. She made the complaint within time and had the text messages as evidence but from the first hearing onwards, she recounted that the ICC members victim-blamed and morally judged her, asking her questions like why she had not shouted and 'gathered' people when her colleague had made physical advances and informally advising her that if she were 'molested' in the future, she should always gather people around her. The presiding officer of the committee repeatedly asked her how she could 'prove' the veracity of screenshots submitted by her in the course of the proceedings and how she could 'prove that molestation occurred' without any eyewitnesses. Additionally, a member interrupted her deposition to tell her that she had observed her 'hugging' male colleagues in the past and warned Zaiba that she would 'expose herself' to men who would wish to take advantage of her if she continued to behave that way. Zaiba later said that the proceedings themselves were arguably as traumatic as the harassment itself and shared that it took her months to move past the 'trial' that she felt she had been put through. Ultimately, the ICC stated that there was insufficient evidence to find the accused guilty of sexual harassment and Zaiba had to resign from the organization.

Something that many workplaces fail to take into consideration, which is evident from Zaiba's story, is that ICCs are comprised of humans, with the same biases, emotional baggage, stresses and uncertainties as many of us. Nandini Bisht, a senior level official, who headed the ICC at her financial services organization, shared in confidence that the ICC members she worked with were 'out of their depth' when deciding sexual harassment complaints fairly. As per her account, ICC issues stemmed from two major sources: lack of confidence, training and expertise of members to make technical decisions on evidence (whether to consider electronic evidence, determining the veracity of evidence presented, etc.) and the hesitation of ICC members to move beyond stereotypical notions of the victim-perpetrator dichotomy and rid themselves of their conditioning, biases and preconceived notions. She shared that although they received a plethora of sexual harassment complaints over the nine years she chaired the ICC, there was always an element of uncertainty, fear and pressure to make the 'right decision', which resulted in arbitrariness when handling many of the trials and a complete lack of 'standardization' in the organization on what would even constitute sexual harassment. The sexual harassment law creates the ICC as an inquiring and adjudicating body, mandates expertise and competence from one member and assumes that the other members have it too, without making adequate enabling provisions to generate that expertise in members.

The gaps in the law, which become glaring during the process of implementation, facilitate an inaccessible system that is centred around judgement, punishment and retribution. At this stage, it must be recognized that the grievance redressal mechanism prescribed in the sexual harassment law, in its current form, can actually be counterproductive to the creation of a workplace culture that is safe, inclusive and open and can also reinforce stigmas around sexuality, sex, professionalism and gender identity. When ICC members are not obligated to 'connect' to a larger workplace culture and remain disconnected from the experiences and narratives of colleagues within their organizations, it results in hearings that are stressful for all parties involved. For the system to work better, it cannot be punitive and retributive in nature and enquiries themselves must be approached in an exploratory, curious manner. The law must be used to further workplace culture and create common voices rather than serving to alienate colleagues and create anxiety and tension in interpersonal interactions.

15

THE MOOT QUESTIONS

Safety

gender dignity

gender/sexual power struggles

organizational diversity

gender roles

myth of gender neutrality

metanarrative on gender

Is there a clear demarcation between dignity and indignity?

Safety and dignity are universal human values where we all know what it means, but beyond the obvious, it becomes difficult to define. If people are asked what makes them feel safe, then the usual responses can be categorized into three—respect of a human being, predictability of circumstances and trust of not being physically, emotionally or psychologically hurt intentionally for the gratification of the other. When asked what makes them experience dignity, some of the common answers are—not being considered lesser than others, being trusted for their intent and integrity and their vulnerability not being exploited. Safety and dignity are often believed to be synonymous or complementary to each other, meaning that we assume that if we feel safe, we will also feel dignified and vice versa. But there is an inherent tension between safety and dignity. For example, in moments of vulnerability, people often seek protection from others perceived to be more powerful than them, with more influence and capital. However, this seeking of protection may need recognition that one may not feel very equal with power holders in such contexts.

Talking about the dignity of gender in the workplace, it becomes both obvious and also ambiguous at the same time. The obvious is when one is not demeaned or humiliated for one's gender or is not sexually objectified. When someone is ridiculed, abused or humiliated for their gender or their sexuality, those actions are easily identified as abuse and exploitation. But there are many attitudes, behaviours and actions which are not as obvious; which may be non-verbal, or a certain tone of speech or what is unstated and unexpressed, wherein gender prejudices or biases may seep. In fact, when men and women have been asked when they experience indignity for their gender, the most common response has been 'in the way someone looks at us', and this is usually said by women or people of sexual minorities. What it indicates is that judgements and attitudes are often latent and non-verbal, people pick up signals of lust, attraction, ambivalence or repulsion from non-verbal cues more often than not. What we, therefore, hear as incidents of harassment or abuse of people for their gender or sexuality is only the tip of the iceberg, which is visible, but what lies beneath (what many characters in the story refers to as 'weird or inappropriate) are intangible experiences, which cannot be 'evidenced'. Thus, it is impossible to list words and actions exhaustively that will cover all possible things that can be said or done which can be unsafe or disrespectful. This makes it impossible for any law or policy to finitely define what can fall under misconduct, misdemeanour and transgression. It can cover the obvious and the minimum—as the POSH law has tried to do.

So what is the nature of tension and power struggle between people of different sexes and genders, that trigger conflict and oppression in different degrees and forms? Such conflicts are not relegated only to organizations, it happens in families and communities and all spaces of life. One way this is often explained is that this is a backlash from men to women's empowerment. As more and more women take on roles that have been traditionally in the male domain, it provokes threat of loss of power amongst men. And misogyny, discrimination against women and insidious forms of abuse and exploitation are an assertion of dominance through the subjugation of women. Discrimination against LGBTQI communities is also of the same vein, where these identities blur the lines between what is male, what is female, what is masculine and what is feminine, and therefore, provokes fear (homophobia) and anxiety. In this narrative, heteronormative men and women along with LGBTQI people get placed in adversarial positions, where the former is seen to be resistant to changes in power dynamics. However, this explanation may not explain why and how situations of conflict do not necessarily always lead to all men defending male gender privilege or impunity.

The other way to explain the phenomena is this. All societies in the world today are in transitional patriarchy. The old order of patriarchy, where the male was the superior sex and the female was considered the inferior sex, has been challenged in most societies and cultures across the world. There is a social agreement that power and authority shall not be conferred onto men for their biological sex and that women have to be equal claimants of power and authority in families, societies and organizations. Societies are increasingly agreeing that heteronormativity (that men and women will be by default heterosexual and biological sex will determine their gender identities) will not be the norm. And that, there must be recognition of the diversity of genders, of sexualities and people of all sexes, genders and sexualities must be included in all spaces, without discrimination.

While this shift may have been agreed upon at a cognitive level, it is yet to be internalized by people, organizations and societies at an emotional and psychological level. Today, in many families, there are gradual shifts in values, beliefs, thoughts and perspectives in not discriminating between girls and boys. We see how, and I am specifically speaking of middle-class and urban communities, earlier de facto decisions of bequeathing property to sons and dowry for daughters is no longer the norm. Many women would not be overly concerned about their daughters learning to cook or sew to earn credits for marriage, and in some cases, parents make their boys learn housekeeping and domestic work. But these shifts are gradual and not drastic. We still largely believe that it is far more important for a boy to be professionally and financially stable than a girl. We see around us that women employed in organizations or entrepreneurs have to multitask and have to balance domestic responsibilities, motherhood and caring for parents-in-law much more than men. So even in our families and homes, in our communities, we are in a state of transition. We are transitioning from an order which put men at the centre and women in the periphery to one where men and women are at the centre. We are moving from an order which said that the key purpose for gender and sexuality is reproduction to an order which accepts that sexuality is a key part of our identities, expression and interpersonal relatedness. We are moving away from the notion that all men must be masculine and all women must be feminine to accepting that there is masculinity in women and femininity in men, which Carl Jung had proposed and one is neither superior nor inferior to the other.

At an organizational level, this transition has been far more scattered. Organizations have created policies for gender equality and non-discrimination, policies for diversity and inclusion but not invested in finding out how that will work. First, it has assumed that people working in the organization would have naturally fit new thoughts, beliefs, values and attitudes as articulated in policies of equalization. Second, the commitment towards being non-discriminatory between sexes and genders has led to equalization of sexes. When it is said that men and women are equal, equality here means equal in power, authority and entitlement. It was said to imply that no sex or gender can have any privilege over the other. However, this has been misinterpreted to mean that men and women are the same, apart from their anatomical differences. Recognizing differences between genders or sex raises concerns of discrimination and the anxiety that the differentiation would lead to segregation. So differentiation between sexes and genders due to bio-existential and physiological differences have been reduced to maternity leaves and separate toilets. This is why one often hears the notion of 'personhood' in organizations, more so from women. This assumption of equalization between genders, through genderless-sexless personhood, is that one must be seen as a person, not with their gender, not as a man or a woman but seen for their expertise, their skills, competencies, commitment, passion and creativity. 'Nothing can be a bigger myth than this', says Sarbari Dasgupta Gomes, a psychotherapist and organizational consultant. 'Our primal way of interrelatedness is through our biological sex and gender. Our first recognition of ourselves is that of a boy or girl and associated with that are roles, work, relationships and attributes. Our relatedness to our parents is also coloured by their gender, as are our interactions with friends and peers, people we are attracted to or repelled by and people whom we admire and idolize. To believe that now, in an organizational space as we step in, people shall be able to neutralize themselves to becoming sexless, genderless entities and relate to each other without any sexual energy, is a delusion', says Sarbari. What this notion of personhood does is to further ignore the fact that when men and women of different genders and sexualities will work together; it will create a sexually charged atmosphere in the workplace, laden with attractions, anxieties and wilful and unwilful transgressions. And if organizations don't engage with this emergent energy in workplaces, it will lead to confusions over propriety, boundaries, legitimacy—what we have read in the case studies.

If issues of gender diversity are addressed only through the lens of transgression, it results in three unintended outcomes. First, it creates a model of oppressor-victim-judge to look at all transgressions, where the complainant is the victim, the accused is the oppressor and the ICC and the organization are put in the role of the judge. ICCs feel ill-equipped to process the complexity of cases. They fall upon POSH law definitions to determine the validity of accusations and look for evidence and the burden to provide evidence falls upon the complainants, which are often difficult and challenging. Over time, the conflict, mistrust and fragmentation grow, pushing operational and middle-level management to resist diversity building pushes.

Second, men often become more defensive and closed to exploration, introspection and growth. Many of their behaviours may leak unconscious privilege and paternalism, misogyny or biases and prejudices. Unless an organization invests in creating safe processes and spaces to foster a reflexive environment, as a prevention strategy, a precursor to actual incidents of the violation, the only time gender and diversity will be engaged with is through accusations of violations. This entrenches the discourse into a battle between genders.

Third, the potential of gender diversity leading to an enabling space for creativity, innovation, dynamism gets lost because gender diversity and inclusion gets caught only in conflict. It prevents an organization from exploring what would it mean for men and women with different identities, to create and shape a space which is not only inclusive, fair and safe but also which differentiates without discrimination.

The argument for gender diversity is not one of social justice alone. There have been multiple studies, including the five-year study reported in *The Harvard Business Review*,[1] which shows that diversity fosters more creativity, innovation,

[1] Alison Reynolds and David Lewis, 'Teams Solve Problems Faster When They're More Cognitively Diverse,' *Harvard Business Review*, 30 March 2017. Available at: https://hbr.org/2017/03/teams-solve-problems-faster-when-theyre-more-cognitively-diverse (accessed on 10 August 2020).

increased productivity and resilience of the organization and business. 'Forward-thinking companies should be looking for ways to employ and empower more women at work—not just as a moral obligation, but also as a sound business strategy',[2] reports the World Economic Forum in a report which says that there is still a wide gap in gender equity in organizations that needs to be addressed and that organizations need to invest for that happen. An article in *Forbes*[3] explains that the five key reasons why diversity and inclusion efforts in an organization fail includes a melting pot assumption, where organizations may continue with the myth of one-size-fits-all approach. So, even while people of different identities are brought in, with their orientations and differentiations, the myth of sameness of all people, regardless of their gender or sexualities results in gender insensitivity, wherein the prevailing norm of thought, values and perspectives may continue to be male and masculine. 'This is the error of disassociation', says Ashok. 'In the pursuit of fighting discrimination, when we choose to ignore differentiation in gender, we end up creating gender insensitive workplaces. In our effort to equalize and explain all differences between men and women as social constructs, we choose to ignore the bio-existential differences in genders. We also forget that we are products of centuries of conditioning and genetic memory and this will manifest in the way we think, we feel and we respond to stimulus.'

---

[2] Vijay Eswaran, 'The Business Case for Diversity in the Workplace Is Now Overwhelming,' *World Economic Forum*, 29 April 2019. Available at: https://www.weforum.org/agenda/2019/04/business-case-for-diversity-in-the-workplace/ (accessed on 10 August 2020).

[3] Glenn Llopis, '5 Reasons Diversity and Inclusion Fails,' *Forbes*, 16 January 2017. Available at: https://www.forbes.com/sites/glennllopis/2017/01/16/5-reasons-diversity-and-inclusion-fails/#40b4c9e50dfe (accessed on 10 August 2020).

LEARNING TO WORK ON GENDER DIVERSITY

Almost two decades ago, organizational consultants Ashok Malhotra and Sarbari Gomes started an experimental lab on gender and identity, at Sumedhas, Academy for Human Context. Ashok is a researcher at heart, a process worker who co-founded Sumedhas and has been studying gender dynamics in organizations and social context for decades. Sarbari, a psychotherapist by training, also a process worker and a fellow of Sumedhas, has been anchoring a lab on gender and identity for Sumedhas for the last 16 years. These labs are experimental and exploratory spaces where individuals and groups work with questions of how they hold gender in their minds, how this impacts their beliefs and values about themselves and others, how this impacts their roles and relationships at families, organizations and communities they are a part of. In the tradition of Sumedhian process work, the philosophy of the lab is to enable people to acknowledge beliefs and values which is held in the conscious and unconscious and for participants to explore what's the kind of man or woman, or trans-identities do they wish to be. The labs draw participants from diverse walks of life, different professional roles—from corporate organizations, social action groups and independent professionals from the media and the arts. Some of the insights gained from the data that has emerged from the labs, are instructive and gives us some direction which may be helpful for corporate organizations and others to learn from.

One of the biggest realizations of the lab has been the myth of gender neutrality. Notions of the masculine and feminine are unconsciously held in the minds of people and translate into conscious or unconscious behaviours in the organizational culture. Interpersonal relationships are coloured by gender—the biological sex of self and the other, what values one ascribes to men and women, masculine and feminine, and what of these are held in pride and honour and what is held as taboo, shame and guilt. Safe spaces for acceptance of our psychological associations with gender create the ground for new explorations and experimentations into new possibilities. Space which prohibits biases and prejudices that one may hold towards gender and identities only fosters denial and repression and heightens guilt, shame and fear. What this reflects is that is for organizations to strengthen gender diversity, interventions must build a safe process of recognizing their mental models of gender and how it reflects in their values, attitudes, choices, pathos and their interpersonal dynamics at work or home. This acceptance without judgement is critical to fostering and enabling any shifts and internalization of new perspectives or values. It also means that for organizations to make a cultural shift, the leadership must engage with this process and not just prescribe righteous policy sanctions meant for others.

ACTIVISM AS AN IMPEDIMENT

The other insight the Sumedhian gender and identity lab offers is that activism often becomes an impediment to change processes for the self and the system. Activism is often drawn from unresolved pain and anger, anguish or trauma that one may have experienced in their own lives or lives of others close to them. Events that they have observed in their childhood or growing up years, conflict and violence one may have experienced in the primary system, workplaces or society. It, therefore, leads to the formation of firm convictions, beliefs and positions, stances, which one dedicates oneself to, often to the extent of proselytism. At some stage, the self becomes a captive of one's ideologies and defence mechanisms in protecting these ideologies become so strong that one finds it difficult to be vulnerable for any exploration, or even acknowledge one's own biases and prejudices. Parts of oneself which do not subscribe to one's subscribed ideologies then are held in shame, guilt and are defiantly closeted. What one must take into consideration with caution is that activism is not solely practised by professional activists. Everyone has an activist in them and when this identity becomes crystallized, it can become an impediment to any exploration or learning. This is pertinent to the issue of how organizations approach to work on gender and sexuality in systems. If the response to sexual violence, abuse or transgressions is only through policies, codes of conduct and zero tolerance campaigns, this heightens the activist identity of the organization. This, then, pushes all of those parts of the organization which may not fit or subscribe to these policies, into a closet, to be held in fear of being ousted, of being punished and shamed.

METANARRATIVE ON GENDER

The third key finding is that there is a metanarrative on gender that is influenced by one's civilizational culture and how that may be distinct (neither better nor worse) from people and communities from other cultures. In other words, there is a distinct pattern in how we hold certain traits in men and women, as being honourable or in shame that is culturally influenced. As Ashok says, 'In the Indian psyche, it may be honourable for a man to be a householder, married and have children and carry forth his lineage and it may be less critical for him to be adventurous, risk loving, athletic to be respected as a man in his society and community, compared to an American man. The idea of masculinity in Bengal may differ from the one in Punjab or Tamil Nadu'.

The Hindu sculptures or deity in temples have male figures which are not muscular, may even be curvaceous and stand in a posture that may seem to be feminine as opposed to Greek or Roman sculptures of men which are far more athletic, muscular and sinewy. The intersections between culture, gender and sexuality have been extensively researched by several academics and social activists as well which all affirm that masculinities and femininities, the ideal and the despicable, the desired and the taboo, vary between cultures and communities. This is important to remember because in multinational organizations, the same policies on gender and sexuality, inclusion and diversity may not work across cultures with the same outcome or process. And therefore, while developing policies or nurturing enabling conditions for culture strengthening towards inclusivity, it would be an important dimension to work on.

THE NOT-SO-FINAL SAY

We live in interesting times. Perhaps every generation that has lived before us have felt the same way about their lives and the times they have lived in. And in that sense, there is nothing better or worse about our times than any of the others. The human saga, the evolution of us as a species and what we see unfolding today in organizations is a part of that process. As is, in the process of evolution, the context never reverts to a past state; it evolves to a new state. Similarly, organizations too will evolve as spaces for people of all genders and sexualities, to work and live and grow in. One can work towards ensuring that this process minimizes violations as much as possible, if not eliminate it. However, the real question for exploration and discovery is, what will organizations in future years from now look like? How will we grapple with all the questions, confusions, dilemmas, hopes and desires we are living with today? How can we live this journey as authentically and meaningfully for ourselves without getting trapped in what should that outcome or evolved state be?

Epilogue

When we started writing this book, we didn't know the shape this book was going to take. We envisaged that the book needs to be written digging deeper into the global phenomena of sexual transgressions being called out, mostly by women, from different industries, against (mostly) men who had been in positions of power over them, and societies across countries responding to them with outrage, defensiveness, cynicism and hopelessness and anguish. From Tarana Burke's first coinage of '#MeToo' in 2006 to October 2017 sexual abuse allegations against Harvey Weinstein, the floodgates opened across the world, across organizations and sectors, to achieve recognition of the magnitude of the problem. In India, the movement started with the Indian film industry and then caught onto academic institutions, the judiciary, corporate and non-corporate organizations and the 2012 law against sexual harassment of women at workplace gathered renewed interest. So, at the onset of writing this book, we asked ourselves—what is really the purpose of this book? Shall we focus on documenting narratives of people who have experienced or reported to have experienced transgressions by virtue of their gender, sexuality and hierarchy in organizations? Shall we focus on solutions for CEOs and chief human resources officers (CHROs) in organizations? Can we, as authors, or researchers, truly claim to have a bouquet of solutions to deal with an issue that is transcultural, complex and has many different forms and shapes, not all of which has necessarily been unpacked from a generic victim-perpetrator narrative?

Once the first draft of the book was written and we shared this amongst organizational leaders, activists and organizational development specialists, one of the demands that came, particularly from managers in the corporate sector was—can you please give us a framework, a clear action plan on what is to be done? While we had discussed this, we had resisted doing so because even though each case study seems to be clear enough to draw inferences and prescribe recommendations, the same case in different contexts and organizations can present different dilemmas. The last thing we wish to do is to create a book of testaments with binaries that may be completely counterproductive in different contexts. For example, let us take the case of a senior manager of an organization—who is married—and has an affair with a junior colleague—a single woman—an affair which when found out by the wife results in him withdrawing from the affair without any closure resulting in the filing of a sexual harassment suit. The company did not have a clear policy on office romances, and there had been no complaints of professional bias against the manager. Whether or not an organization will prohibit office romances or choose to see it as a personal matter regardless of the persons' marital status must emerge from a negotiated value judgement by people working in that organization. If people in the organization belong to a society and culture where extramarital affairs are seen as a personal choice, then an organizational prohibition may be seen as moralistic interference and the issue may become more covert, illicit and toxic. In our research that we have shared with you in the latter analytical chapters, we find that ineffectiveness of organizational policies addressing vulnerability and transgressions is a top-down approach and not being participatory enough in its framing and development. So, we can tell you clearly what does not seem to work—a consultant-developed sexual harassment policy that is based on fear and threat of indictment, without adequately engaging on the issue of gender and sexual diversity, safety and trust. What hasn't worked thus far, and probably will not work ever, is a behaviour focussed list of do's and don'ts. Because what constitutes transgressions, as we have seen, is more on intent than action, the same words and actions can mean different things depending on the relationship, trust and familiarity between two people concerned, and propriety of actions and words is culture-specific. For example, staff at the Gatwick Airport have been prohibited from using terms such as 'love' or 'darling' based on complaints from people of different cultures for whom the terms may be offensive, but for the British, the terms do not suggest impropriety. With more and more globalized and multicultural teams, focus on words and actions leads us to a hyper-anxious chiselling of behaviours to achieve political correctness without addressing the basic issues of understanding, trust and abuse of power.

However, we do understand that we have an obligation to the readers—to offer our suggestions on how to take things forward in their own organizations. What we can say with absolute certainty are the first four steps, which are not activities but key structural scaffolding to facilitate strengthening of a system to become more gender-diversity friendly, and safer workplace that will have its own processes of preventing abuse of power and exploitation.

1. The issue of gender and sexual diversity needs to be framed as a part of the diversity and inclusion (D&I) portfolio in an organization. We strongly advise against treating sexual harassment as a stand-alone issue under the POSH policy disconnected from the D&I policy. Building organizational cultures that is inclusive to women, trans-people, people of sexual minorities and men, and learning to discern between distinctiveness and discrimination is the best way to approach prevention

of sexual harassment and abuse of power in the workplace. Gender diversity and inclusion is not an outcome, it is a process; it is not a result to be achieved in a checklist of representation in recruitment quotas or extending spouse benefits to same sex couples only. As we have heard the various representational characters from different organizations say—'We feel safe when we are seen, heard and understood.' There may be several studies that have argued for demographic diversity in organizations, and it has become a pill that everyone has swallowed without checking, testing and validating in their own organizations. Therefore, rather than treating D&I interventions as politically correct actions for social justice, CHROs and CEOs must create a culture of curiosity in the organization to assess and audit periodically and find out 'What are the intended and unintended consequences of diversifying workforce demography in our organization? How are people in the organization experiencing diversity? How do they experience safety and trust between men and women, people with different orientations? How are people reconciling their personal values and organizational values, where there is a fit or where they are divergent?' These are questions that one does not consciously think about in daily life and may often experience them in encounters and interfaces with colleagues. Many organizations have found creative ways of triggering questions and conversations on some of these issues not only through workshops and outbound trainings but also through online content that provokes people to think, discuss and debate on issues of gender, sexuality, ethics and safety. These programmes help contributing to 'prevention of sexual harassment'—a concept that is barely articulated in sexual harassment law in India.

2. Leaders leading the D&I action may benefit from coaching and experiential labs on gender and identity to design interventions on how the system holds gender and sexuality and enables unfolding and unleashing of potential of the system to engage on the issues. One big potential for exploration and dialogue in any system is—What does it mean for people to be men and women in the workplace? As we have explained in this book, something which we find as a recurrent theme, is that the notion of 'personhood' that is non-gendered and asexual and an entity that must be recognised by its role, skills and competencies, is a myth that many have internalized without questioning their actual experience. Any suggestion of distinction raises concerns of how the distinctions may lead to discrimination, and invariably work against women, and this concern is legitimate. For example, the argument that women have more biological, psychological and social demands as a mother has been used against them to keep them from promotions or to prevent them from being given challenging roles in organizations. Or saying that men's bodies have more physical strength and therefore are to be deployed in physically challenging jobs have worked against interests of women who are still barred from many jobs by many organizations. So, one understands the anxiety over accepting distinctiveness. The challenge, therefore, for organizations is to co-hold distinctiveness without being discriminatory or abusive to perpetuate prejudice. This requires skills and expertise and therefore, organizations must recognize the need to build its expertise amongst its leaders.
3. The sexual harassment policy ought to be one of the tools linked to the D&I policy that specifically responds to complaints and grievances. If norms and values in

the organization are well developed under the gender and sexual diversity vertical, the management and ICC members will find it easier to work through issues that they currently have no common understanding on and will rely less on personal morals and biases. One of the findings from our research is that ICC members have spoken about need for orientation and training in not only the law but more importantly in skills of interview, investigation, analysis and in perspective building on issues of power, sexuality and gender dynamics in systems. Activists or social workers from non-profits invited into ICCs are, often, not 'experts' and are as lay as the rest. Some of them who have worked on domestic violence or sexual violence issues may bring perspectives that may have its benefits as well as liabilities.

4. Many companies in India have not restricted their sexual harassment policy for only women; however, very few of them have explored the issue of sexual harassment of sexual minorities in their POSH policy, something we recommend. With decriminalization of sexuality choices of adult persons in India, and many companies taking active measures to recruit LGBTQI people and extend health benefits and spouse entitlements to their partners, it is critical to remain alive to tensions. Rather than stigmatize homophobia as an illness, one must accept that having grown up in patriarchal and heteronormative cultures (where sex has been normalized between heterosexual married people, social and behavioural codes for men and women have been distinctive and separate), everyone may consciously and unconsciously carry beliefs, fears and anxieties towards breaking of these social and moral codes. For an organization to become more inclusive and respectful to

diversity, recognizing and engaging with these feelings associated with what has been socially and morally repressed for decades or centuries will help build the psychological maturity of the system and truly make it inclusive through a process.

The COVID era has triggered a very significant shift for organizations and workplaces, one of which is the sudden jump to remote working, working from home. While this may have been triggered by an external provocation that forced organizations and people to this new arrangement, it has created a tremendous jolt to the whole notion of the workplace. The workplace is no longer primarily restricted to offices and allied spaces but has broadened to include the home, the house of the person where he or she lives. Companies are identifying new ways of communication between management and employees, for teams to coordinate and engage with each other, to cooperate and collaborate. Many companies have come to believe that this shift has actually made work processes and engagement much more efficient and will do away with offices even post-COVID when there may be no threat of the virus. CHROs and HR professionals are speculating if this will lead to reduction of sexual transgressions and complaints, though the counter argument is that hierarchy and abuse of power will play out differently, the nature of tension and transgressions may be different and even more complex if much of what gets reported is outside any organizational premise. With lack of physical interface and communication becoming virtual and impersonal, very purposive and transactional, many of us foresee a new set of challenges that will emerge in terms of building organizational culture and identity. Most CHROs have reported differential challenges that women and men are facing in work-from-home, lockdown phases where women disproportionately have to manage much more housework than their husbands or other men in the family. In some of our client organizations, CHROs have reported that 90 per cent of women wish to return to office to work because they are overworked, exhausted and fatigued having to manage the housework and meet official demands. On the other hand, 40 per cent of men have reported that they find it more convenient to work from home not having to commute large distances and having work flexibility. Womens housework is not only restricted to the domestic chores of washing, cleaning and cooking but also to child care and elderly care. It is too early to say how issues of power, sexuality and gender dynamics will change in a post-COVID era, but what is certain is that it will, if companies shift to a remote working culture.

About the Authors

Roop Sen is a researcher at heart who is passionate about asking questions—the right questions that allow better and deeper insights and, sometimes, delightful answers. Roop has always been curious about how our gender identities, social norms and power structures impact the lives and opportunities available to different groups of men and women and the non-binaries.

In his engaging conversations, whether over endless cups of coffee with friends or at his workshops, he facilitates inquiry into how our childhood experiences and primary relationships shape our lenses for looking at ourselves and others, in organizations and society.

He is a founding member of Sanjog, a non-profit, and Change Mantras, a consulting firm. As an activist, he supports people's movements against gender-based violence in society and the organized crime that profits from it. As an organizational consultant, he works with client systems in India and other cultures on gender, organizational culture and identity politics to strengthen resilience in organizations.

Roop is a fellow of Sumedhas, an organization that delves into the human context, where he co-anchors the Gender and Identity Lab with Sarbani Gomes and Ashok Malhotra. 'From being an activist whose lens on gender was focused on gender-based violence, the labs have been a great learning experience on learning to look at ourselves with compassion without collusion,' says Roop.

The one who asks questions does not lose the way. And with this book, Roop's pursuit is to evoke and provoke questions and discussions on issues that may be currently blurred but need to be moved into the spotlight so that we do not really lose the way home to a gender-just world for all.

Uma Chatterjee is postgraduate in applied clinical psychology from the University of Delhi. She started multiple organizations throughout her life—from a special guidance clinic and laboratory for children with special needs in Chandigarh, Sanjog—an organization for the emancipation of survivors of sexual violence and slavery—to Change Mantras, a leadership development firm.

A 'compassionate leader' is how Uma's colleagues describe her. While she holds strong convictions about her views and does not hesitate to make unconventional choices in life, she is equally empathetic to people who have different views and beliefs than her own.

Uma is perhaps best known for her work with young women and men in India who have survived gender violence and caste exploitation. She has invested a better part of the last decade fostering and mentoring the youth to mobilize, collectivize and organize themselves—to connect with each other and support themselves to heal and emancipate. 'Empowerment cannot be bestowed by the privileged to disadvantaged, nor can saviours and crusaders rescue the fallen. The best way to heal the hurt is to listen and share, our vulnerabilities, our fears and anxieties, and those parts of us which we feel ashamed to reveal, even to ourselves,' says Uma.

A mother of a teenage daughter, she sees how, in so many ways, her daughter's context, peer culture and worldview are different from hers. At the same time, the connection between her own mother, herself and her daughter, in their desire, their struggles and their hopes as women connects their worlds. This book, Uma hopes, will evoke 'grey' conversations on identity, gender and sexuality. For it is in the messy grey areas where we find complexity, compassion and the truth.